WATCH THEM GROW

THE FASCINATING SCIENCE OF ANIMAL BEGINNINGS

CARRIE A. PEARSON

M Millbrook Press / Minneapolis

To all the babies of the world—especially mine—may you grow, thrive, and inspire. And to Cyndee, thank you for exceeding the challenge!

Special thanks to author and educator Jessica Fries-Gaither for reviewing and commenting on the science content.

Millbrook Press™
An imprint of Lerner Publishing Group, Inc.
241 First Avenue North
Minneapolis, MN 55401 USA

For reading levels and more information, look up this title at www.lernerbooks.com.

Illustrations on pages 17, 20, 21, 23 by Laura K. Westlund.

Designed by Kimberly Morales.
Main body text set in Johnston ITC Std.
Typeface provided by International Typeface Corporation.

Source Note

18 Ryan Lister, quoted in David Stacey, "Gene Switch Makes Us Look Like Our Animal Cousins," Phys.org, March 1, 2016, https://phys.org/news/2016-03-gene-animal-cousins.html.

Library of Congress Cataloging-in-Publication Data

Names: Pearson, Carrie A., 1962– author
Title: Watch them grow : the fascinating science of animal beginnings / Carrie A. Pearson.
Description: Minneapolis : Millbrook Press, [2026] | Includes bibliographical references and index. | Audience term: juvenile | Audience: Ages 9–14 Millbrook Press | Audience: Grades 4–6 Millbrook Press | Summary: "How do animals develop the traits they need to survive? Discover the many ways animals grow before they are born." —Provided by publisher.
Identifiers: LCCN 2024048838 (print) | LCCN 2024048839 (ebook) | ISBN 9798765627464 library binding | ISBN 9798765659236 epub
Subjects: LCSH: Embryology—Juvenile literature | Epigenesis—Juvenile literature
Classification: LCC QL971 .P38 2026 (print) | LCC QL971 (ebook) | DDC 612.6/4—dc23/eng/20250204

LC record available at https://lccn.loc.gov/2024048838
LC ebook record available at https://lccn.loc.gov/2024048839

Manufactured in the United States of America
1-1012026-52130-4/14/2025

CONTENTS

INTRODUCTION

BABY BEGINNINGS

Caution! Cuteness alert!

Downy, peeping ducklings. Wide-eyed chimpanzees. Long-legged foals with velvety noses . . . We can't help but love looking at baby animals.

But do you ever wonder how animals grow *before* they're born—or hatched?

It's hard to imagine how baby animals develop since they're tucked safely inside their mom or curled up in an egg. We know it isn't magic. We can't wave a wand, and *POOF*, a miniature Asian elephant appears.

No matter how big or small, whether it lives on land or in the water, every animal, including a human, goes through similar events to become what it is.

But hold that thought. To start at a baby's beginning, we need to get small—really small.

Two-month-old Eastern chimpanzee

YOU'RE SO CUTE!

In 1943 Austrian scientist Konrad Lorenz developed the concept of baby schema (called Kindchenschema in German), a set of face and body features that humans—including young children—find cute. Animals with a round face, high forehead, big eyes, and small nose and mouth are the cutest to humans.

Why is cuteness important? It turns out cuteness is not only important but is also a lifesaver. Here's why: Infants' faces provide a lot of information about their age and health. Scientific studies have shown that a part of our brain is activated when we see babies. Looking at them gives us a sense of reward and other positive emotions. These feelings make us want to pay attention to or take care of babies. This is crucial because baby mammals, especially humans, are altricial (al-TRISH-ul)—they need adult care to survive.

It's not just about cute babies. Natural selection is at work here. In natural selection, animals that are better suited to their environment survive and have babies. Their bodies and behaviors can slowly adapt or evolve over generations as environments change. With baby schema, as mammals evolved over time, babies with these face structures received better care. Those babies were more likely to grow up, reproduce, and pass their lifesaving baby faces to the next generation.

Lorenz introduced an important concept to the world. Today, researchers can use a technique called geometric morphometrics to study faces. Scientists place points on digital pictures of faces and create maps of the shapes. These "face maps" can be measured and compared using computer software programs.

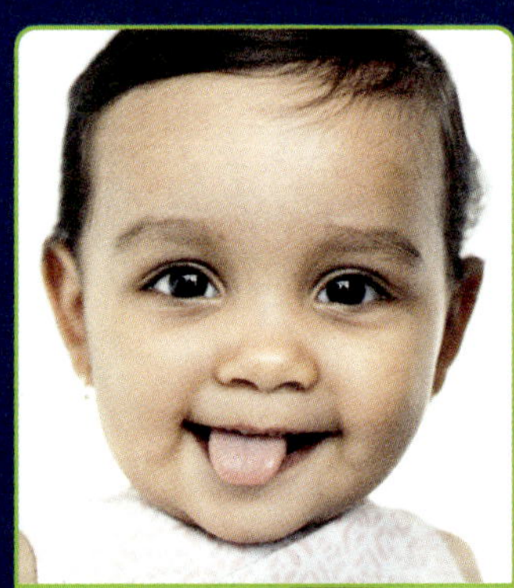

Although baby schema exists across many altricial animals, how animals respond to it differs. Baby schema motivates some animals (including rats) to care for any baby of their kind, whether it belongs to them or not. Some animals, such as sheep, only feed and care for their offspring. Humans have a "generalized cuteness response"—we are motivated to care for any cute baby, no matter who that adorable face belongs to.

This drawing compares the adult (*left column*) and juvenile (*right column*) features of a human, a rabbit, a dog, and a bird. The juveniles have larger foreheads and eyes and smaller chins than the adults.

You are going to read about a lot of different animals species in this book. But what exactly are species? They are groups of animals that are similar enough to reproduce successfully and create offspring that can also reproduce. For example, a poodle and a labrador retriever (both members of the dog species *Canis lupus familiaris*) can produce a puppy that can grow up and have its own puppies. Subspecies live in different geographic areas but are similar enough to reproduce. Dogs are a subspecies of wolves (*Canis lupus*).

CHAPTER 1

POV: YOU'RE A CELL. WAIT! YOU'RE AN ELEPHANT?

Take our baby Asian elephant, for example. Although it may weigh about 200 pounds (91 kg) at birth and 6 tons (5.4 t) when fully grown, it starts so small that we would need a high-powered microscope to see it. This playful pachyderm begins as one *cell*, the smallest unit of life.

All living things, all organisms, are made up of cells.

Some organisms (such as bacteria) are one-celled, or *unicellular*. One cell does everything the organism needs to survive.

Elephants (and other animals, including humans) are more intricate. They develop many different kinds of cells. They are *multicellular*.

Imagine how many cells are working together to keep this Asian elephant mother and calf alive!

But even if an organism has many cells, how can it grow into something as large and complex as an elephant? Or a human?

It is possible because living bodies are made up of many systems that work together.

And it all starts with cells.

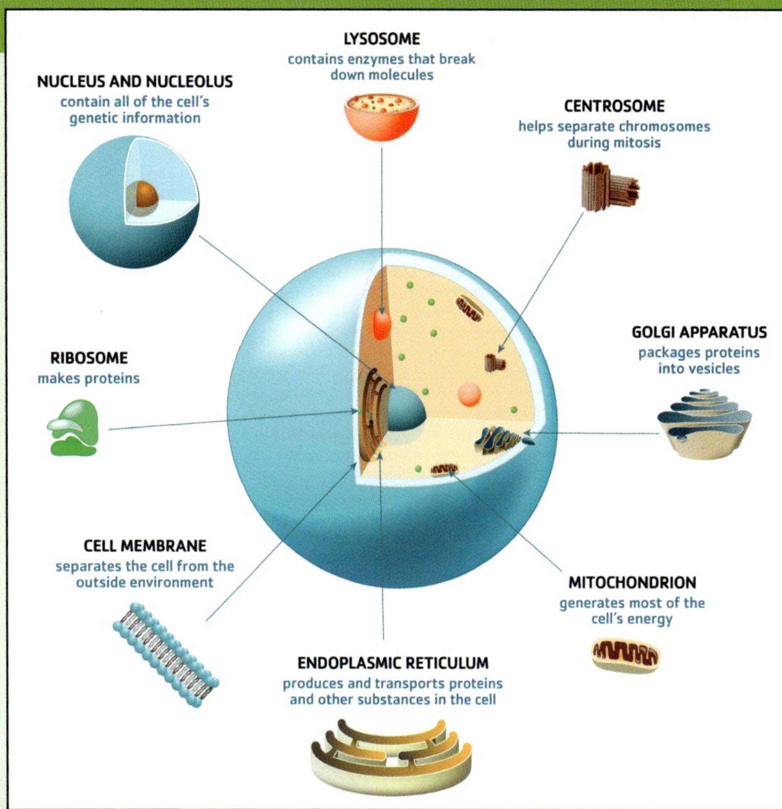

Animal cells include multiple structures that have different functions.

Each cell is like a mini city with different structures with their own duties. For instance, the outer coating of a cell, the *cell membrane,* is like a wall around a city. It has channels that sometimes allow entry and exit. The mitochondrion in a cell is like a city's power plant. It generates energy to power the cells' actions. The nucleus of a cell is like a city government. It makes the rules and tells the cell what to do. And cells have other structures too.

A CELL IS SMALL, BUT TOGETHER, THEY'RE MIGHTY!

A typical animal cell is at least thirty thousand to one hundred thousand times smaller than the period at the end of this sentence. Scientists estimate that an average man's body will have about 37.2 trillion cells (written with zeros, that's 37,200,000,000,000 cells!). Elephants really put the "multi" in multicellular. An average African elephant will have about as many cells as one hundred adult humans.

GETTING SMALLER: CHROMOSOMES, DNA, AND GENES

Every cell's nucleus contains threadlike *chromosomes* that provide directions for building the organism. The main job of chromosomes is to transfer these directions from one cell to the next.

Chromosomes come in different numbers and sizes in different organisms. But, just like socks, chromosomes usually come in pairs.

A human cell typically has twenty-three pairs of chromosomes, or forty-six chromosomes. Twenty-two pairs (uncreatively named "1," "2," "3," up to "22") give instructions for how a body will grow, develop, and function. The remaining pair, the sex chromosomes (named "X" and "Y"), determine our biological sex and some other functions. Generally, females have two X sex chromosomes in each cell (XX), while males have one X and one Y (XY). Sometimes, a person may have extra sex chromosomes, or one might be missing, so other patterns, such as X, XXX, XXY, and XXYY, can also occur.

Chromosomes are made of deoxyribonucleic (dee-AHK-see-ri-bo-new-klee-ik) acid (Go ahead; say it out loud. You've got it.), or DNA. DNA has two strands that are tightly coiled on a skeleton of proteins, similar to a tiny, twisted ladder. This structure is known as a double helix.

CHROMOSOME PAIRS

Each species has its own number of chromosome pairs. But having more chromosome pairs doesn't always mean a species is more complex. For example, pigeons have 40 pairs, while humans have 23 pairs. Here are more interesting chromosome counts:

A female southern red muntjac deer has only 3 pairs.

A tiger has 19 pairs, while a common carp has 50 pairs.

A striped Grevy's zebra has 23 pairs, while a domestic horse has 32.

That baby elephant? It has 28 pairs.

Speaking science: The number of chromosomes for an organism having chromosomal pairs is shown as 2n: X. For example, human chromosomes are shown as 2n: 46, or 2n=46, meaning we have 23 pairs or 46 total.

THE HUMAN GENOME PROJECT

Scientists have mapped the sequence of genes (known as a *genome*) in humans. This accomplishment, called the Human Genome Project (HGP), took thousands of specialists worldwide over thirteen years to complete. They discovered that the human genome contains between twenty and twenty-five thousand genes! And each gene has a duty, such as the human gene LEP on chromosome 7, which helps regulate our hunger.

The HGP and biomedical teamwork that followed helped scientists understand how organisms develop and function, from the tiniest to the largest parts. For example, in humans, the gene SMARCAD1 on chromosome 4 is involved in forming our fingerprints. Gene CA1 on chromosome 8 controls the thickness or density of the femurs in our upper legs, which are our biggest bones.

The HGP found genes associated with diseases, which help researchers learn about the genetic start of conditions such as cancer, diabetes, and heart disease. Now, specialists can develop treatments and medications, even some that are targeted for the genes in one person's body. The HGP also pushed the boundaries of genetic technology, which led to new ways of "reading" genes. Researchers are using that technology to map the genomes of other animals. This leads to a better understanding of how their bodies work, how to care for them, and how to treat their illnesses.

These long strands contain chemical building blocks organized in a specific order called a sequence. Small sections of that sequence are called genes. Genes guide traits, features, or functions. For example, genes code for how an organism fends off disease (its immune system), eye color, and, if it has hair, how curly or straight it will be.

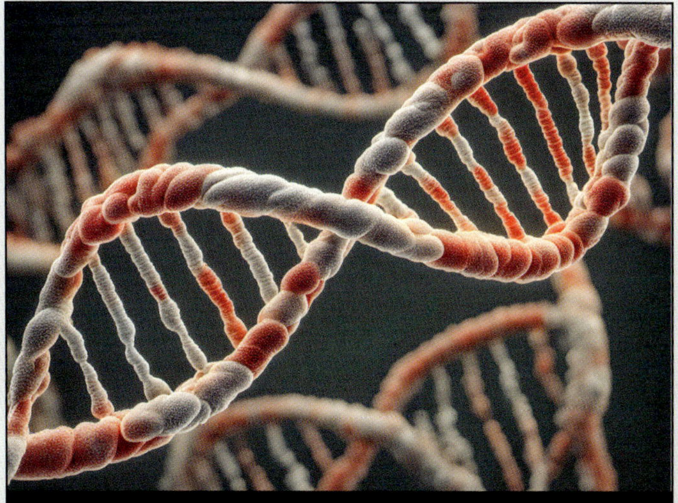

All living organisms on the planet have DNA. Whether in a human, a plant, or an animal, DNA is the same substance. It's the sequence of the chemical building blocks that make each organism unique.

MAKING MORE (MITOSIS) AND MAKING HALF (MEIOSIS)

You might be thinking, okay, I understand the structures of cells, but how does the elephant develop so many kinds of cells? Here's how:

Multicellular organisms such as animals have two main types of cells: somatic cells and gametes. Most cells are somatic and form the body's tissues and organs, such as skin, muscles, kidneys, and lungs.

When somatic cells divide and replicate, we call this *mitosis*. Mitosis is good for growth, repair, and maintenance of the body. It happens every second of every day. We can't feel mitosis, but we can see an example when we heal from a scrape or cut. New skin cells form to replace the damaged ones and fill in the cut. Cells also divide so living organisms can grow.

Here's how it works: Think of somatic cells as mini cities. Imagine that a city (cell) wants to cover more territory. "I'm so cool. Why not have two of me?" So, it copies, or *duplicates*, its structures and moves its outer wall (cell membrane) inward until two separate cities

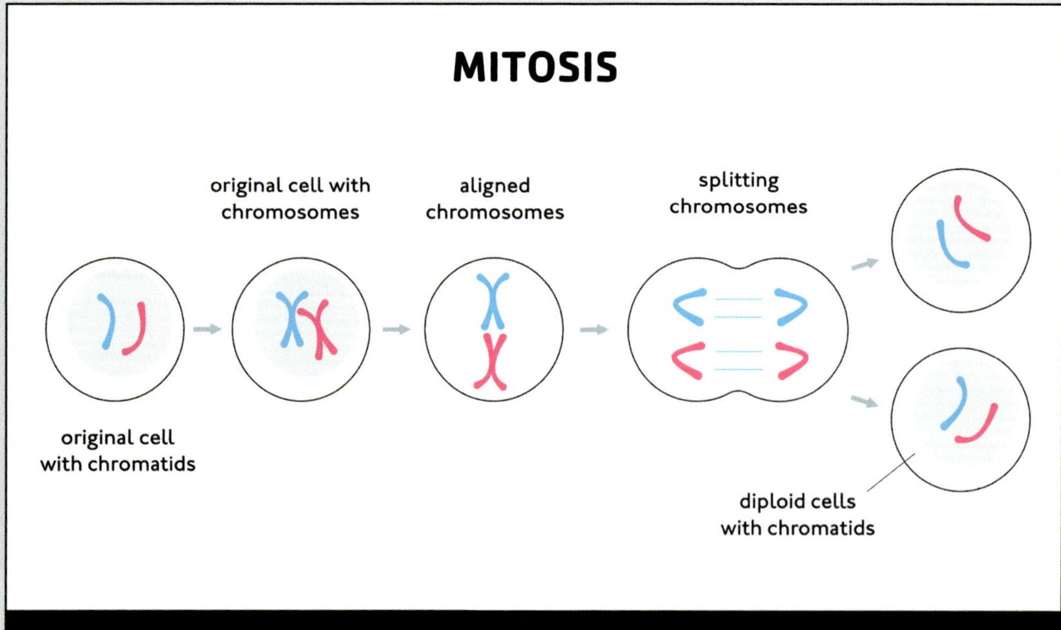

Mitosis is the process that body cells, such as those in skin, muscles, kidneys, and lungs, undergo to make exact copies of themselves. In this illustration, only two chromosomes are shown. But this process occurs for all of the chromosomes in a cell.

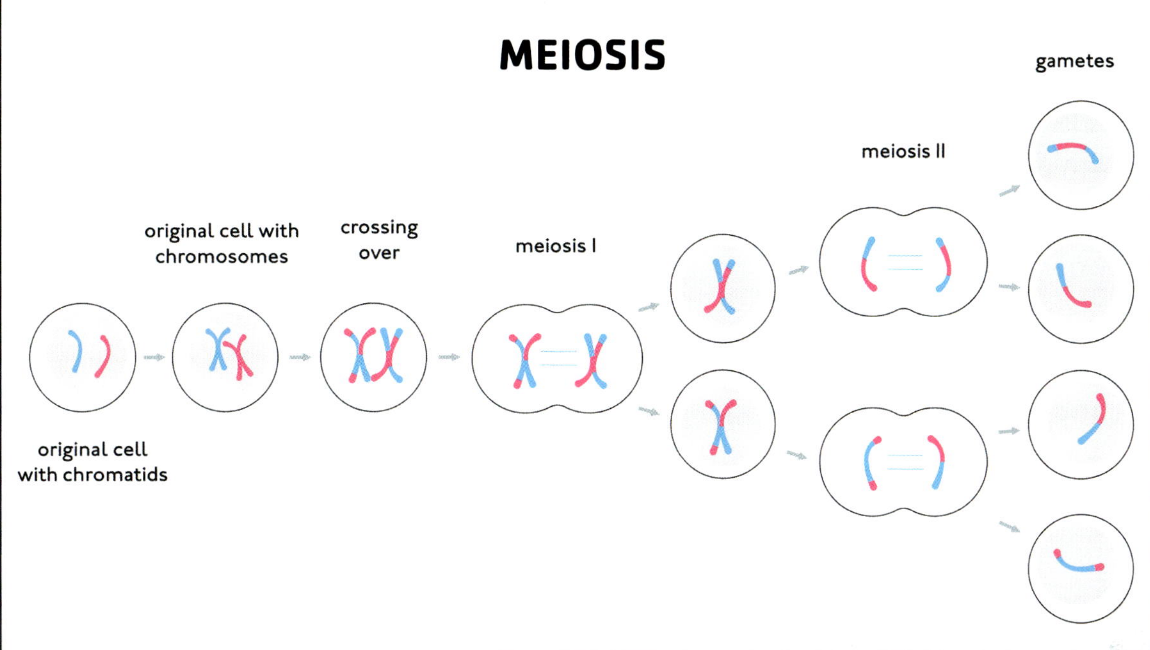

Meiosis is the dividing process for reproductive cells, such as ova and sperm. The resulting cells contain half of the chromosomes as the parent cell.

(cells) are formed. This way, each new cell gets the same structures, including two copies of each chromosome.

The dividing cell is the *parent*, and the two new cells are *daughter* cells. Mitosis's superpower is producing daughter cells that are genetically the same as the parent cell, including two sets of chromosomes. These are *diploid* cells ("dip" sounds like "*dup*-licate").

The other main type of cell, *gametes*, are reproductive, or sex, cells. In animals and humans, female gametes are called *ova*, or *eggs*, and male gametes are called *sperm*. Gametes carry only one copy of each chromosome. They are *haploid* cells ("hap" sounds like "half").

Gametes are formed through *meiosis*, another type of cell-dividing process. Meiosis creates daughter cells with half as many chromosomes as the parent cell.

The gametes produced through meiosis aren't identical to the starting cell or to one another. Each gamete has a unique combination of genetic material, which is important for creating offspring.

GAMETE, MEET GAMETE

Most animals, including our Asian elephant, reproduce sexually—the biological father provides sperm, and the biological mother provides ovum, or eggs. When sperm and eggs join, this is called fertilization. Fertilization is the starting point of a new individual with its own genetic blueprint. The offspring will get half of its chromosomes from the biological mother and half from the biological father. Because of this unique combination, each offspring will be genetically distinct. Here is an exception: If the fertilized egg splits, identical babies (twins, triplets, or more) could occur.

Offspring from sexually reproducing individuals inherit two sets of chromosomes with genes—one set from their biological mother and

THE FORCES OF CHANGE

Meiosis, natural selection, and evolution help species survive in a changing world. Here's how: Imagine a game in which living things must adapt to changing rules to win, and these three forces drive the changes.

- **Meiosis:** DNA mixes and creates new combinations during cell meiosis. This is similar to shuffling a deck of cards to get a unique hand every time.
- **Natural selection:** Determines which animals survive and reproduce based on how well they fit into their environment. For example, if the climate becomes hot and dry and the ground changes color due to this dryness, animals that blend in with the new color will be camouflaged and hidden from predators. These animals survive and reproduce. Living things don't have a choice in natural selection, and it can take many generations for natural selection to appear. But even small changes, such as a shift in fur color from dark to light, can contribute to the survival of a species.
- **Evolution:** Over time, the traits that help animals survive, such as blending in with a new environment, become more common. So, if lighter-colored mice are less likely to be eaten because they match the dry, light-colored dirt, more light-colored mice will have babies, passing on their light fur to the next generations.

In the actual game of life, meiosis mixes up the traits, natural selection picks the best mix for the environment, and evolution ensures these traits continue, helping species adapt to new challenges.

one set from their biological father. The genes from each parent line up in the same order on these chromosomes.

Do you see the word *gene* in *gene*ration? Genes are passed from one generation to the next.

An *allele* is one pair (or a series) of lined-up genes. Alleles are different versions of the gene and can be the same or different. Here's an example: For the gene that determines eyelash length in elephants, Mom might contribute an allele for long lashes, and Dad might contribute an allele for short lashes. The trait the elephant shows (long or short lashes) depends on the alleles passed down.

Because each parent provides one set of chromosomes, the offspring will be somewhat like the parents, but not exactly. This can easily be seen in humans. Imagine a family photograph. Siblings who share the same parents will have some of the same traits, such as eye color, but will not look identical to their parents or each other.

THE OG SELFIE

Specially trained scientists, called geneticists, can isolate and create a photograph of chromosomes in our bodies. This image is called a karyotype. Many steps and special equipment are needed to complete a karyotype. Generally, scientists isolate one cell (usually a blood cell) and apply dye to stain the chromosomes within it so they can be seen under a microscope. When stained, the chromosomes look like strings with light and dark bands. They are organized by size, counted, sorted, and

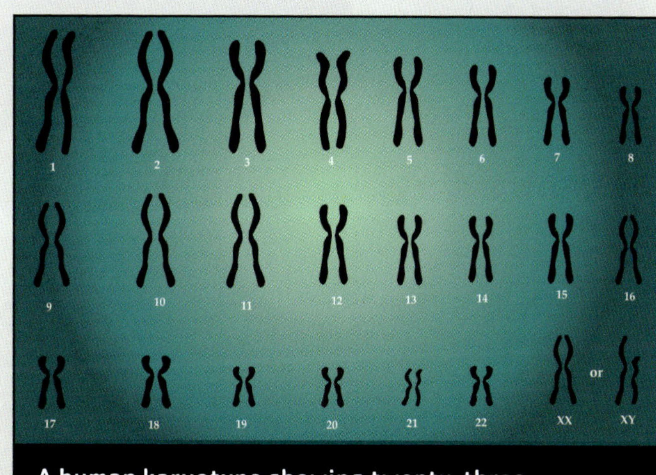

A human karyotype showing twenty-three chromosomes including an XX or XY chromosome

analyzed. Finally, they are arranged by number, and a digital picture is created. Karyotypes can be used to identify health problems or look for genetic issues when adults are considering having a baby.

GESTATION STATION

Now that we know about cells, chromosomes, DNA, genes, alleles, and traits (whew!), we can return to the events every animal goes through to become what it is.

Sexual reproduction: Ovum, or eggs, are stored in the female's ovaries and travel to fallopian, or uterine, tubes in preparation for mating. When a male and female mate, sperm is transferred from the male through its penis that has been positioned near or into the female's vagina.

Fertilization: When a sperm and an ovum merge, they become a single *fertilized* cell. This new diploid cell—a zygote—contains all the genetic information needed to become a new animal with traits similar to its biological parents.

Gestation: Once that zygote is formed, it needs a place to live and grow. The period during which an animal develops inside its mother or egg before being born or hatching is called *gestation*.

Different species of animals have different gestational processes. There are three main categories: egg laying, live birth (such as our Asian elephant), and hatching from eggs inside the mother, followed by a live birth—more on this to come.

Are you wondering if we're at the cute part?

Not quite yet. But we're getting closer.

Embryo: Back to our zygote. It isn't unicellular (one cell) for long. Thanks to mitosis, it divides into a bundle of cells that will eventually become one whole organism. These cells remain very small. So even though the number of cells increases, the overall size isn't getting much bigger yet. At this point, the cells are *stem cells*, meaning they could become any cell in the body, much like toy building blocks can become a tower, rocket, or house.

In the case of our elephant and other mammals, the stem cell bundle travels through fallopian tubes to the uterus and implants there to grow and become an *embryo*.

Within days, the stem cells begin to *differentiate*, or become particular types of cells. These differentiated cells become part of developing structures that form the body.

Eventually, when the embryo reaches the gastrula stage, it becomes a cuplike structure with three layers of cells:

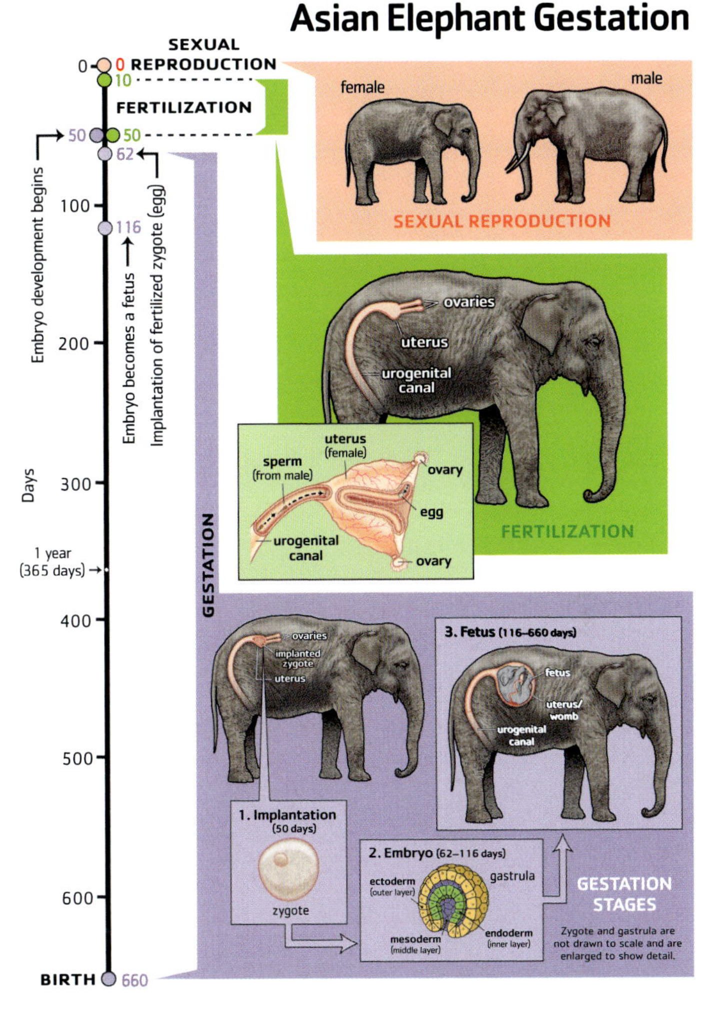

Elephants have the longest known gestation of any mammal, lasting about two years. This allows their complex brains to develop before birth.

The inner layer, the endoderm, forms many of the internal linings of the body and certain organs, including the colon, stomach, intestines, lungs, liver, and pancreas.

The outer layer, the ectoderm, develops into the outer layer of skin, hair, mammary glands (where milk is produced), and the nervous system.

The middle layer, the mesoderm, develops into all other body tissues, including the heart, muscle system, reproductive and urinary system organs, bones, and bone marrow (where blood is produced).

This is when our baby elephant begins to take shape!

EVEN DIFFERENT ANIMALS BEGIN ALIKE

Embryos of vertebrates (animals with a backbone), from a white weasel to a blue whale to a human, look strikingly similar at an early stage of their growth. This is called the phylotypic (fi-loe-TIP-ick) stage, or period.

A scientist named Karl Ernst von Baer first described this stage in the 1800s. But it was partly due to an error in recordkeeping in his laboratory! Von Baer collected embryos from different animals to investigate their development but forgot to label two species. When he tried to match the embryos with the correct species, he couldn't tell them apart. This lab "failure" helped him realize how alike embryos are across different species at a certain point in their development. His work also led to a better understanding of how embryos develop.

Although it's easy to spot the differences between animals such as a rhino and a rabbit at birth, von Baer and other scientists' work of that time showed that vertebrates have a shared ancestry. Modern-day scientists who study embryo development, including Ryan Lister, a professor at the School of Molecular Sciences at the University of Western Australia, are investigating why.

Lister was interviewed about his work, and he described results from some of his team's phylotypic stage research comparing frog, fish, and mouse embryos: "It was thought that vertebrates showed such similarity during this developmental period because that was when the fundamental structure of the body was being set up. Correct establishment of the body plan and organ formation at that early stage is so critical to life that the molecular processes underlying it have remained very similar despite millions of years of divergence between these species."

So, even powerful forces such as evolution and natural selection haven't changed the critical early stage of development in animals with a backbone.

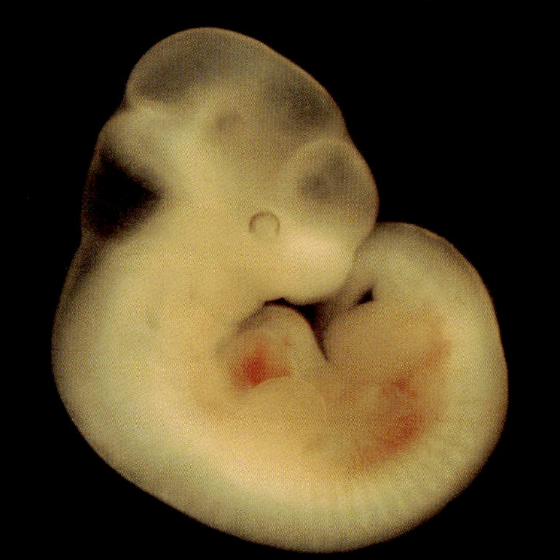

Top: A Caribbean tree frog growing inside a transparent egg. It is one of very few species that fully develops before hatching.
Bottom: Mouse embryo, day eleven of development

Fetus: When a mammal has developed basic body structures and begins to have body parts that look like an adult of its kind, it is called a *fetus*. This would be a little less than four months of gestation for an elephant. The fetus develops inside the uterus within its mother's abdomen.

Sometimes, development only takes about nine weeks, such as for a puppy, or sometimes two years, such as our elephant!

WHAT'S FOR DINNER? HOW DEVELOPING ANIMALS GET NOURISHMENT

It takes a lot of energy to grow from a single cell to a fully formed baby ready to enter the world. Many important nutrients, such as proteins, fats, and natural sugar called glucose, are the fuel for growth. Each animal species has its own system to deliver nutrients while their babies develop. Some systems are unique (we're looking at you, great white shark!), but many aspects are similar.

Placental Mammals

Most mammal fetuses grow inside a flexible, pancake-shaped organ called the placenta, which develops in the mother during gestation. One side of the placenta connects to the fetus's belly through a tube of tissue called an umbilical cord, and the other side connects to the mother's uterus. The placenta temporarily acts as the fetus's lungs, digestive system, and kidneys until those systems can function.

Placental mammals with umbilical cords all have a "belly button," which is the scar left when the cord is detached from the fetus after birth. Can you imagine the size of an Asian elephant's belly button?

Inside the placenta, the fetus is surrounded by a membrane called the amnion, which is filled with amniotic fluid. Amniotic fluid starts as water from the mother's body. Eventually, the fetus swallows the liquid and makes urine inside the sac. Amniotic fluid also contains nutrients, infection-fighting antibodies, and chemicals made by the body called hormones that instruct how the body grows. This vital fluid also protects animals from injury in the womb and helps regulate their temperatures.

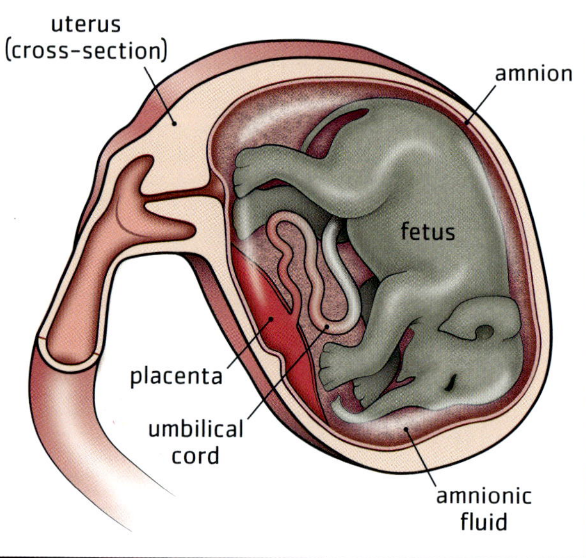

The amniotic membrane is filled with amniotic fluid. It surrounds the fetus and acts like a water balloon, cushioning the baby and keeping it safe as its mother moves.

Birds

All birds lay hard-shelled eggs that contain developing embryos. Some development has already begun when a fertilized chicken egg is laid. But the progress only continues if the egg is kept at an optimal temperature (about 99.5°F, or 37.5°C, for most birds) and doesn't get dried out. In the wild, most bird eggs are incubated, or kept at the right conditions, by the adult birds' body heat.

Eggs come in all shapes, sizes, and thicknesses and include a shell or covering that wraps the contents.

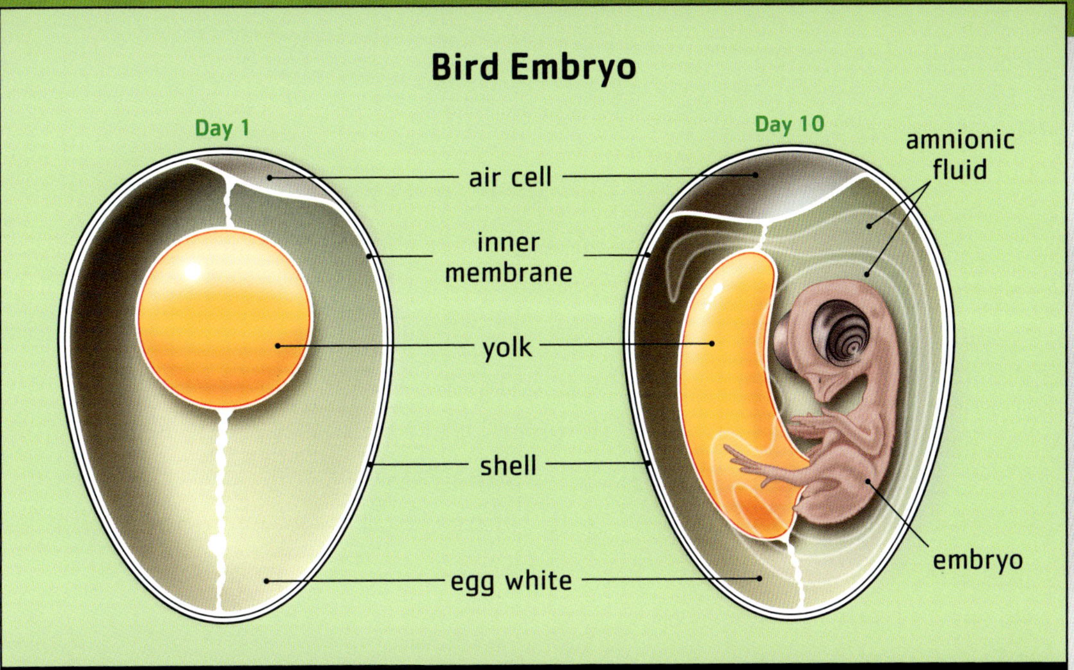

Hard-shell eggs are mostly made of calcium carbonate, the same material found in some rocks. This makes shells rigid yet slightly flexible.

Hard-shelled eggs can protect the embryo through difficult conditions, such as changes in weather. But even these eggs have tiny holes called pores. Pores allow the transfer of oxygen into the egg, and waste, such as carbon dioxide and excess moisture, out of the egg. Membranes inside the eggshell protect the embryo from bacteria and help prevent too much moisture loss. Meanwhile, the yolk sac develops inside these membranes, providing the embryo with minerals, vitamins, fat, and protein while it grows.

Did you know scientists think birds evolved to develop their babies outside their bodies (in eggs) because carrying a baby inside would make the female too heavy to fly? Here's another interesting fact . . . the egg yolk can sustain a chick even after it hatches. During the final days of incubation, the chick draws what remains of the yolk into its body. This gives it extra nutrients to survive a few days after hatching.

Monotremes

Monotremes are mammals that develop inside eggs that their mothers lay. Platypus embryos develop inside a soft, leathery egg in the mother's oviduct (a tube from her ovary where her ovum is stored). The yolk sac in the egg provides nutrients similar to a bird's egg. But because the platypus egg is softer, it can also absorb certain nutrients from the mother's body.

Later, the mother lays them in a nest through her cloaca, an opening between her hind legs. The cloaca is the end of a tract, or tube, inside her body that also expels urine and feces. The embryos keep growing inside the eggs for another ten to twelve days. Nutrients in the egg yolk keep them alive. Finally, they hatch and lap up pools of their mother's milk or suck on the fur near it for three to four months until they can eat independently. The milk oozes through the mother's mammary gland ducts (a channel for fluids to pass through in the body) because platypuses don't have nipples like other mammals.

A baby short-beaked echidna rolls on its back. This species is a monotreme like the platypus.

Marsupials

Marsupials are mammals that are born at an early development stage. Then they stay very close with their mothers to finish developing. Before birth, a tammar wallaby gets nutrients from a yolk sac in its mother's womb. But there's no connection to its mother like a placental mammal. As soon as the tammar wallaby consumes its yolk, it has to be born to stay alive and develop much more in her pouch.

Live-Birth Reptiles

Most reptiles hatch from eggs their mothers lay. But the slow worm, mamushi snake, and copperhead snake are born live. These embryos develop inside soft eggs in the mother. When they've used all the nutrients in the egg yolk, they hatch inside her uterus (or oviduct) and continue growing with the help of the mother's nutrients. Later, they are born live and ready to survive on their own.

A female copperhead snake gives birth to live offspring. The young snakes can fend for themselves as soon as they emerge from the placenta, which is the blood-tinged covering seen on the snakelet.

Live-Birth Fish

Most fish hatch from eggs outside the mother. But some fish, such as the great white shark, are born alive. Great white shark embryos begin as fertilized eggs in the mother's oviduct. Each soft and flexible egg holds a developing embryo and a yolk sac. The yolk sac is rich in proteins and fats that are transferred to the growing embryo. From the oviduct, the embryo

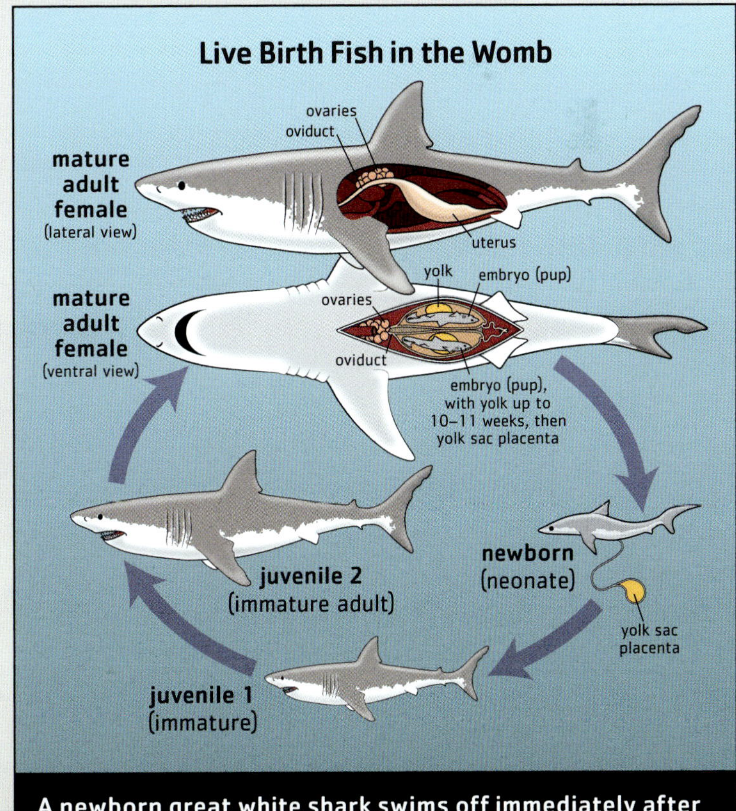

A newborn great white shark swims off immediately after birth so it doesn't get eaten by its mother.

moves into one of the mother shark's two uteruses. Each uterus secretes "uterine milk," a liquid with nutrients that help the embryo develop body parts, such as teeth and fins, that it will need immediately after birth. The great white shark embryo also consumes unfertilized eggs in the uterus, which the mother continues to produce to feed her developing pups.

No matter how long animals grow *inside*, or gestate, the most important part of their development is preparing their bodies to live *outside*.

On their own, their lives will depend on their ability to move, sense things around them, and ingest (eat and drink). Why are these abilities important for an animal's survival?

Let's find out and watch them grow—before they're born.

SCIENCE IN ACTION: SAVING ANIMALS THROUGH A MICROSCOPE

Carly Young is a scientist who works at the San Diego Zoo Wildlife Alliance in San Diego, California. She's an expert in reproductive sciences, so she knows a lot about how animals create more of themselves. At the San Diego Zoo Wildlife Alliance, her job is to help save endangered animals. Young uses techniques such as in vitro fertilization (IVF), where ovum and sperm are combined outside of the female's body and then the embryo is placed in a uterus, either of the same female or another, to develop. IVF can be used to help people have babies. Young uses this and other techniques to help endangered animals have healthy offspring.

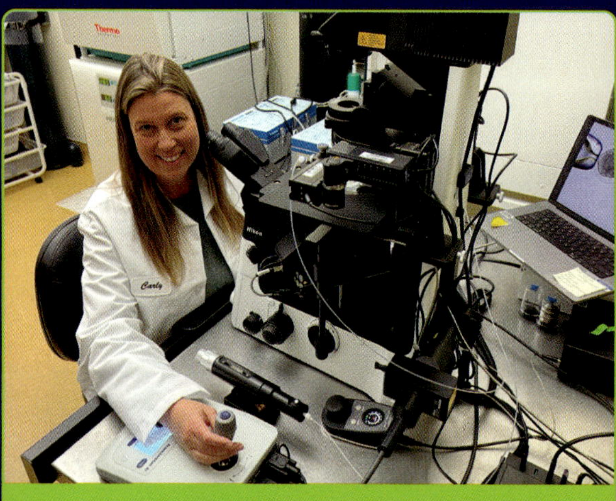
Carly Young works on the micromanipulators on the inverted microscope.

One of her most important projects is working to save the northern white rhino, a subspecies of rhinoceros that is functionally extinct. This means none are left in the wild and very few live on Earth. Two female northern white rhinos are left. Najin and her daughter Fatu live in a sanctuary in Kenya and are protected by guards twenty-four hours a day. Since there are no living male northern white rhinos, the animals cannot reproduce naturally.

Enter Young and the team of people around the world who are using microscopes and science to save them.

One strategy is to fertilize white rhino ovum in the lab with white rhino sperm collected from the last male northern white rhino. Then, if it is viable, or healthy enough to grow, place the embryo in the uterus of a *southern* white rhino that will act as a surrogate, or substitute mom. This would be possible because the northern white and southern white rhinos are subspecies.

Young uses her skills as a microinjectionist to practice and perform the crucial procedures needed to save the northern white rhino. She also works on saving endangered reptiles such as lizards and snakes by freezing and preserving their sperm so it can be used in the future.

Some equipment Young, an animal embryologist, uses include the following:

- **An anti-vibration table.** This heavy table sits on four air pistons to make it "float." The table keeps her working area still despite footsteps and air flow in her lab.
- **An inverted microscope.** Its design is the opposite of a common light microscope and allows her to see living cells (such as sperm and ovum) in conditions they need to survive.
- **A micromanipulator.** This robotic device allows precise movements that she can't perform using her own hands.
- **Microtools.** Controlled by joysticks on either side of the microscope, microtools are tiny glass pipettes (tubes) with tips as small as the diameter of a human hair. Microtools allow her to hold a single ovum without damaging it and pick up one sperm and inject it into the ovum. With the microtools, sperm and ovum are magnified four hundred times!

A one-day-old southern white rhino calf stands near its mother at the Leofoo Village Theme Park in Hsinchu, Taiwan. Southern white rhinos born in captivity (in zoos and sanctuaries) typically weigh about 100 pounds (45 kg) at birth!

CHAPTER 2

MOVE IT! BODY PARTS DESIGNED FOR MOVING

Movement can mean life or death for many species, even for a slow-moving sloth. Whether they climb, creep, dig, dive, soar, swim, jump, slither, or glide, animals must move to do the following:

These lion cubs are less than a year old. But they are adapted for life on the move in the Maasai Mara National Reserve in Kenya.

A herd of wildebeest sprints across the savannah during the great migration in the Serengeti Plain. These animals can reach sprinting speeds of 50 miles (80 km) per hour. Their speed helps them outrun predators.

- **Find food.** Most animals move to search for food. Predators chase prey, and plant eaters (herbivores) move to find plants to graze on.
- **Avoid being food.** Movement allows potential prey to escape from predators. This might involve running, jumping, flying, hiding . . . any form of movement to keep from becoming lunch. For many species, moving together is safer than moving individually. In these cases, an animal that can't move could be left behind to fend for itself.
- **Locate the right habitat.** Animals move to find somewhere they can thrive, a place that provides the right combination of food, water, and shelter and where they don't have too much competition for resources.
- **Stay warm or cool.** Animals move to find a more favorable or safer environment. They might seek shade when the temperatures soar or burrow underground to avoid freezing.
- **Find mates.** Some animals, such as migratory birds or salmon, travel long distances to return to their breeding grounds when it is time to mate. Others, such as deer, might roam to locate a mate during breeding season.

An animal's ability to move, whether crossing a road or crossing a continent, is essential for survival. Let's check out how three animals develop body parts designed to get them moving.

SHORT-TAILED FRUIT BAT

What's going on inside? Short-tailed fruit bats welcome their wings.

Bats are the only mammals that can truly fly rather than soar. This takes special wings. Bat wings enable these animals to catch delicious insects, evade predators, thermoregulate, and migrate—almost all the crucial activities bats need to do when awake!

A short-tailed fruit bat starts to grow its wings after about five weeks in the womb. First, the bat sprouts two sets of limbs. But one set, the forelimbs, grows long, fingerlike bones. Then, the wing "skin" called *patagium* grows between the finger bones and attaches to the bat's body. This thin membrane allows the bat to scoop air and get lift when it flies.

Species: *Carollia perspicillata*
Common name: Seba's short-tailed fruit bat
Baby name: pup
Type: placental mammal
Chromosomes: 2n=20
Range: northern Argentina to southern Mexico
Gestation: about four months

A Seba's short-tailed bat flies on powerful wings.

Number of wombmates: usually none

Did you know? Although a short-tailed fruit bat weighs only as much as a nickel when born, its wings are heavy for its body size. Why? Unlike birds, bats can't launch themselves from the ground. Instead, they have evolved to roost upside down and fall into flight. And while birds have hollow bones, bat wing bones are solid. That extra weight, or mass, helps inertia work in their favor. Inertia is a force that explains why something moving stays in motion (or something still stays still) unless another force acts on it. When it is time for a bat to roost, it flies toward its hanging place, and just before reaching it, the bat pulls one wing slightly closer to its body. Much like a twirling ice-skater changes the speed of their revolutions by pulling in or extending one leg, a tiny movement of the bat's wing while in motion reorients the bat (inertia at work!) and puts it into the perfect upside-down roosting position. When it's time to leave its perch, the short-tailed fruit bat is ready to take off in an instant.

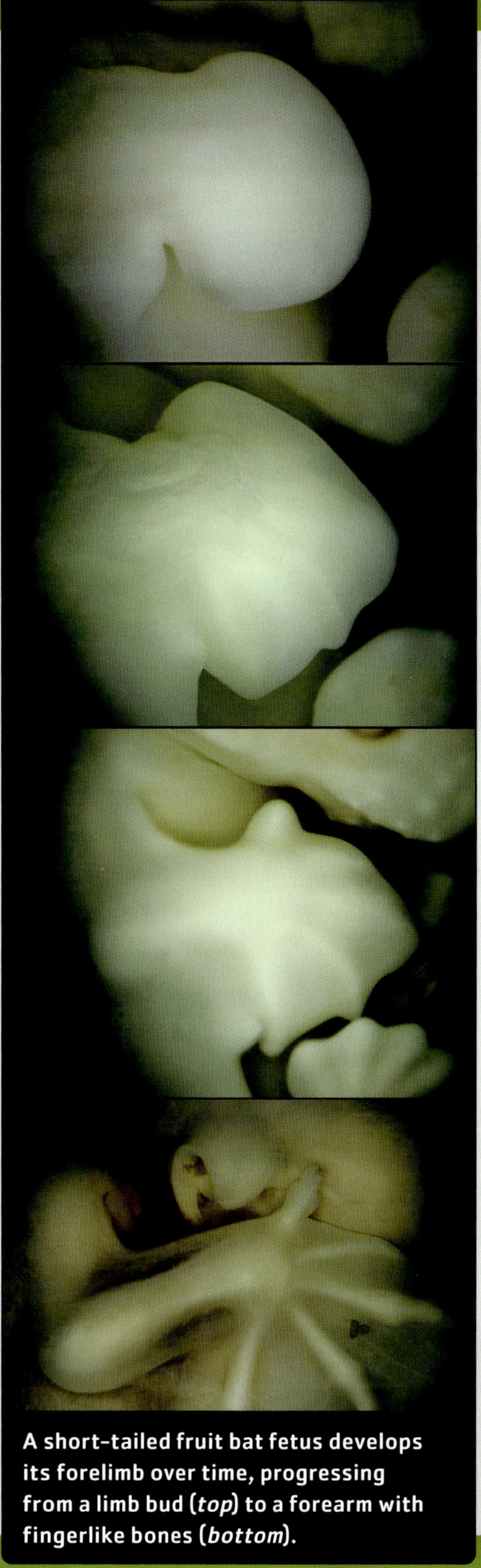

A short-tailed fruit bat fetus develops its forelimb over time, progressing from a limb bud (*top*) to a forearm with fingerlike bones (*bottom*).

PANTROPICAL SPOTTED DOLPHIN

What's going on inside? Pantropical spotted dolphins finish their flukes.

A dolphin's tail, or fluke, helps them escape predators and strike fish for dinner. Unlike fish, which move their tails sideways, a dolphin moves its fluke up and down. Once the dolphin and its fluke are fully grown, this flexible, powerful body part propels it up to 18 miles (28.9 km) per hour through the water!

The fluke begins as a tube shape like all mammal tails (including the tails human fetuses have for a short time!).

But in the third month of the dolphin's development, the left and right sides of the tail grow out to form a diamond shape. As the fetus grows, the sides of the fluke grow even farther. The fluke finishes up as a flattened triangle. It stays bendable and tucked under the fetus's body to save space in Mom's uterus during development.

Dolphins communicate with their flukes too. They hit the water surface with their tail, making a loud sound that can travel far. This behavior is called a tail slap and may be a sign of aggression, a signal to leave the area or to attract other dolphins' attention.

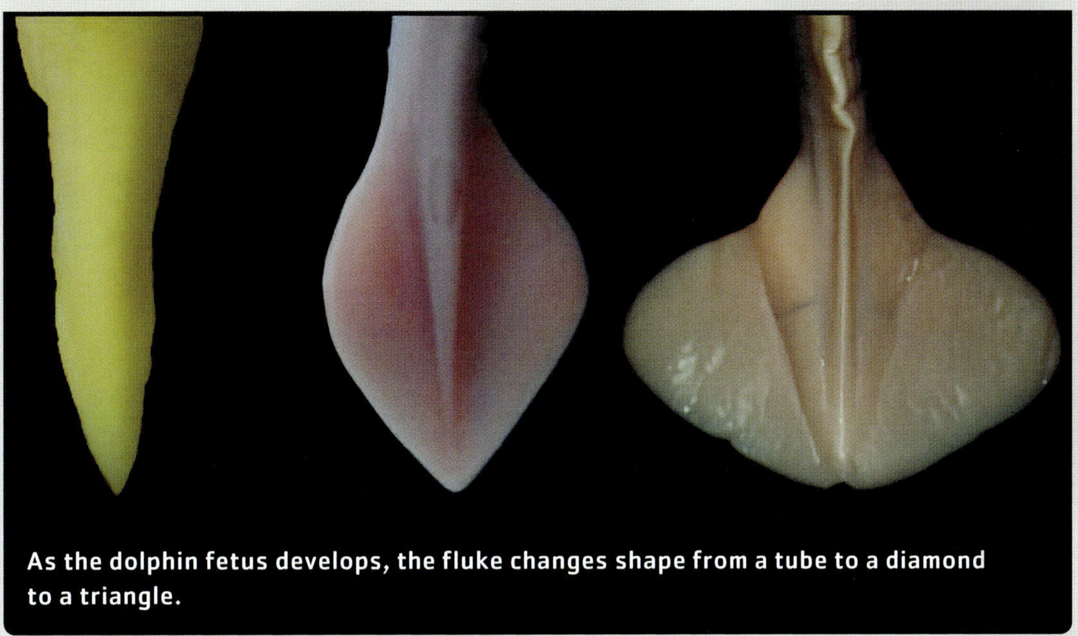

As the dolphin fetus develops, the fluke changes shape from a tube to a diamond to a triangle.

Species: *Stenella attenuata*
Common names: Pantropical spotted dolphin
Baby name: calf
Type: placental mammal
Chromosomes: 2n=42
Range: oceans around the world
Gestation: one year
Number of wombmates: usually none
Did you know? Dolphin calves use their flukes to swim immediately after birth. But they need help from their mothers to keep up with the pod (family group). For several months, calves swim in their mothers' slipstreams. This column of still water is naturally created behind adult dolphins when they swim, much like a wake behind a moving boat. Baby dolphins tuck into their moms' slipstreams where there is less resistance and a smoother flow of water. Then the calves can expend less energy as they swim and keep up more easily.

SLOW WORM

What's going on inside? A slow worm builds a backbone.

This sleek creature looks like a snake but is actually a lizard—without legs. Unlike snakes, they have movable eyelids, ear openings on their heads, and a rounded tongue instead of a flat forked tongue. Most animals can use their legs to push against the ground for leverage to move. But a slow worm uses its strong backbone, or *vertebrae*, to push against objects or against the ground to help propel it forward. Joints connect the individual vertebrae like door hinges. These joints, plus muscles attached to the backbone, allow the slow worm to bend and curve its body to move like a snake.

The vertebrae form early in gestation but begin as cartilage like our ears. As the slow worm develops, most vertebrae ossify, or become bone. The backbones closer to the slow worm's head become bone first, and the vertebrae closer to its tail take longer to develop. But by the time the slow worm is born, its long backbone is ready to help it slip under cover, find food, and escape.

Meet the slow worm. Although it looks like a snake, it is actually a lizard without legs.

Species: *Anguis fragilis*
Common name: slow worm
Baby name: neonate, or juvenile
Chromosomes: 2n=44
Habitat: Europe (except for the far north, islands, or the southern Iberian Peninsula and southern Greece) and east as far as western Siberia and Iran, the only reptile found in the Outer Hebrides.
Gestation: two to three months
Number of wombmates: usually six to twelve
Did you know? The slow worm lizard, like most lizards, can practice autonomy. It can sacrifice its tail or a portion of its tail to a hungry predator. When a slow worm's tail is pulled, a piece separates from the rest of the tail and continues to wriggle and thrash! Hopefully, the predator is fooled and focuses on the "tail" while the rest of the slow worm quickly and quietly slides to safety. What about the rest of the tail? It will grow back but isn't detachable again.

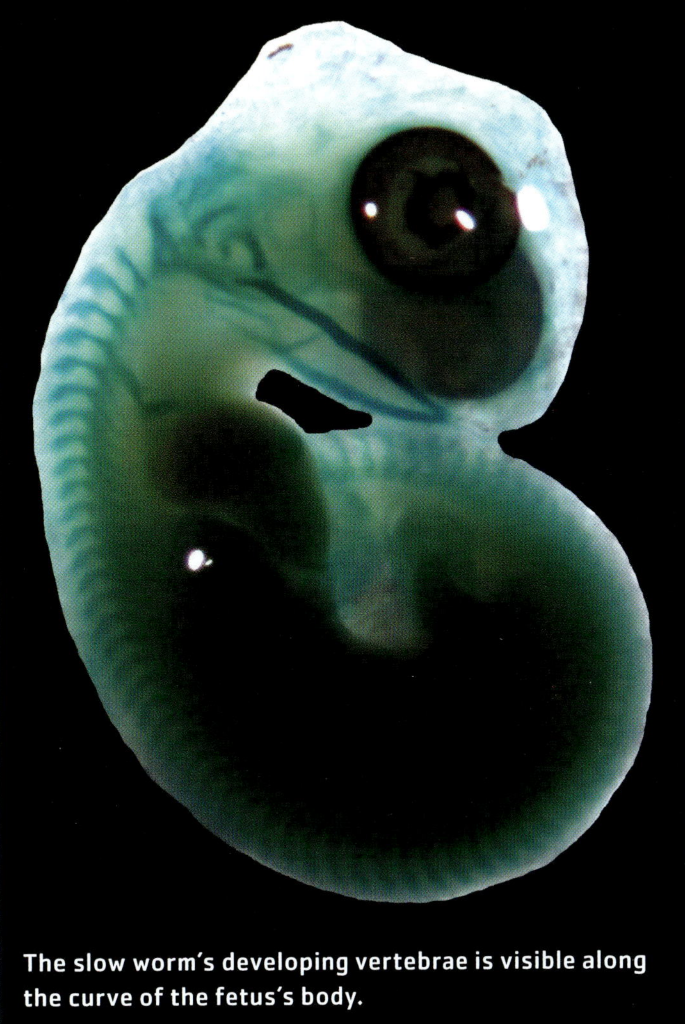
The slow worm's developing vertebrae is visible along the curve of the fetus's body.

CHAPTER 3

MAKING SENSE: BODY PARTS DESIGNED FOR SENSING

Humans have five basic senses to gather information (you know these: sight, hearing, touch, taste, and smell), with sensory organs and nerves that transmit that information to our brains.

We understand how we perceive the world around us. Our senses make sense to us. (Get it?)

But imagine a world with more senses. Many animals have senses far beyond humans' abilities. For example, bats use echolocation to sense their surroundings and find food by sending out sound waves and listening to the echoes they produce when they bounce off objects. Elephants use low-frequency sound waves or infrasound to communicate from many miles away. Some snakes use special heat sensors to find warm prey.

Fennec foxes live in arid climates and use their very large ears to listen for prey under the sand. Once found, they dig quickly and capture their meal.

Scientists are still learning whether extra abilities like these are connected to animals' main sensory organs or if these abilities come from additional organs or systems.

No matter what the animal is, its senses are vital for doing these things:

- **Finding food.** Predators and prey use their senses to locate food and track food sources.
- **Avoiding predators.** A quick getaway depends on sensing a predator before—GULP!—it's too late.
- **Finding mates to reproduce.** Finding the right mate at the right time often depends on a keen sense of smell and pheromones, or scents that motivate behavior.
- **Communication.** Whether animals are alerting others in the herd to danger, helping young navigate their habitat, or

THE *HOMO SAPIENS* (HUMAN) SENSORY EXPERIENCE

The animal kingdom shares some sensory abilities but not all. Here's how humans' five senses work:

INCOMING! Ears, eyes, skin, mouths, and noses—also known as sensory organs—collect incoming information from the world, such as noises, light, taste, touch or pressure, and the chemicals that make up a smell. Each sensory organ has different receptor cells that detect stimuli or information from the environment. For example, touch receptors in the skin detect pressure and temperature. The stimulus is converted to electrical signals or nerve impulses that are transmitted to the spinal cord and brain through sensory nerves.

Different parts of the brain process and interpret the signals depending on where the signals come from. Then the brain instructs the body on how to respond. Sometimes, processing happens quickly through the spinal cord and sends a response right back to the muscles. This is called a reflex. (If you touch something too hot, you'll pull your hand away before your brain processes the pain.)

finding lost members of the group, senses are necessary for sending and receiving messages.

- **Interacting with the environment.** Animals use their senses to learn about their surroundings and evaluate their and their offspring's safety.

Animal survival depends on their ability to gather and use data from their environment to their benefit. Let's discover how three animals develop body parts designed for sensing their world.

HOUSE MOUSE

What's going on inside? House mice work on whiskers.

When whiskers touch objects, they help the animal gather information about the environment. Whiskers are essential for house mice because, as a species, they have limited vision.

Mouse whiskers begin to develop about ten days before birth when ridges form on each side of the snout. Over the next few days, the

One house mouse mom can produce 15 to 168 pups per year depending on its living conditions. That's a lot of mouths to feed.

ridges grow into a pattern of five horizontal (side to side) rows with one vertical (up and down) row closer to the eye. Each row includes follicles, or cavities in the skin, where the whiskers form. They will emerge about two days before birth.

After birth, whiskers grow longer. They are slightly curved and tapered from bottom to top like a candle. These important features help the baby mouse move about its world, stay safe, and find food.

Species: *Mus musculus*
Common name: house mouse
Baby name: pup
Type: placental mammal
Chromosomes: 2n=40
Range: every continent in the world except Antarctica
Gestation: nineteen to twenty-one days
Number of wombmates: three to fourteen pups per litter
Did you know? Whiskers aren't typical hair. They are vibrissae, thin filaments that grow out of different follicles than regular hair. Vibrissae follicles are much deeper and are surrounded by pockets of blood that amplify vibrations. Whiskers are made of keratin, the same substance as our hair, our fingernails, and chickens' beaks. But mouse vibrissae are

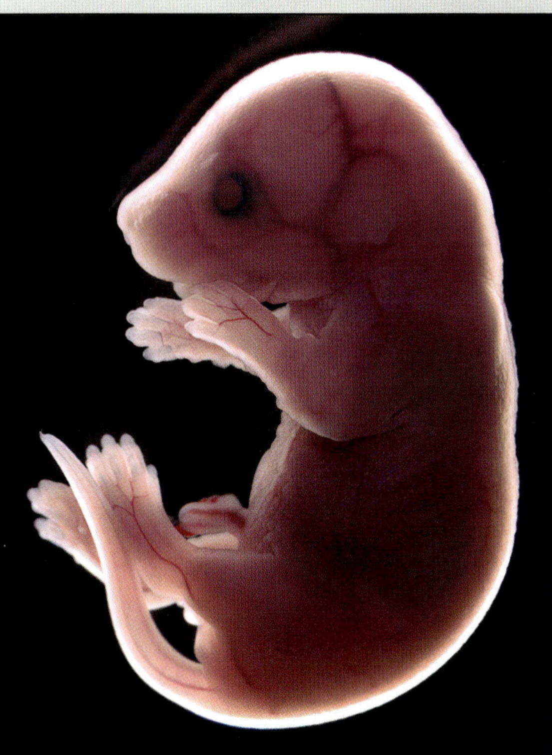

Top: Rows of whisker follicles are lined up early in gestation.
Bottom: A house mouse fetus about two days before birth. Its whiskers are present but hard to see. They will lengthen just before the pup is born.

flexible strands, each contributing tactile, or touch, information. There are two kinds of whiskers: long and short. House mice move their long whiskers to sweep, or whisk, an area. Short whiskers don't move but instead help mice figure out what an object is.

DOMESTIC DOG

What's going on inside? Domestic dogs sharpen their sense of smell.

Dogs rely on their noses to explore their surroundings, learn new things, and remember past experiences. Their sense of smell is powerful, ranging from ten thousand to one hundred thousand times more powerful than a human's. These furry friends can sniff out drugs, explosives, and even detect illnesses in people, such as COVID-19, certain cancers, and changes in blood sugar levels due to type 1 diabetes. All this super smelling starts before birth. Puppies remember some scents they were exposed to while in the uterus!

One reason dogs effectively communicate through smell is because odors stay in the environment. Dogs can gather information without being physically close or interacting directly with whatever left the odor.

The beginning structures of the fetus's snout, the nasal pits, can be seen by day twenty-seven—about halfway into their gestation. By day thirty-nine, this beagle pup has developed the alar folds, or slits, on the side of its nose. When a dog inhales, air passes through the nostrils. The oxygen keeps the dog alive, and the dog analyzes the air for scents. The air is pushed down and out of the alar folds when the dog exhales. This way, old air is separated from new air and scents are kept clear.

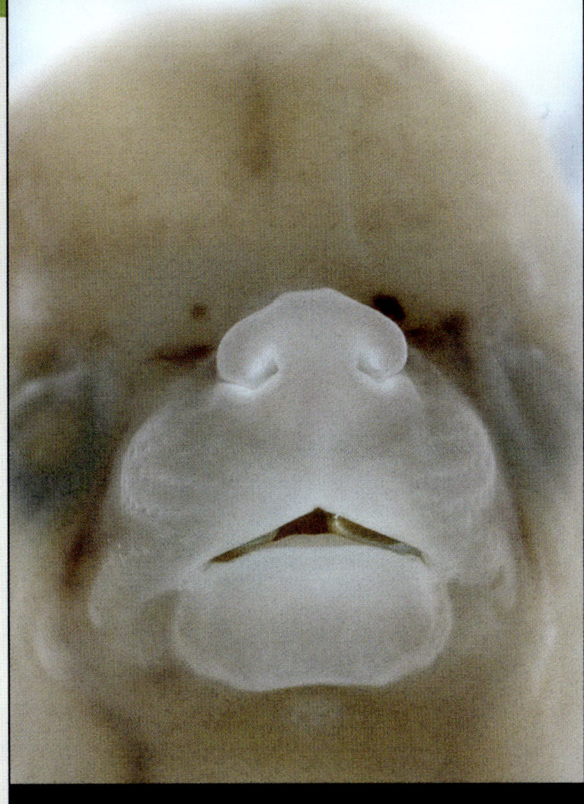

The dog's sense of smell develops early as seen on this thirty-nine-day-old beagle fetus.

Species: *Canis lupus familiaris*
Common name: domestic dog
Baby name: puppy
Type: placental mammal
Chromosomes: (golden retriever) 2n=78
Gestation: about three months
Range: primarily in Europe and North America but can be found in homes around the world.
Number of wombmates: eight to twelve puppies
Did you know? Sniffing and smelling aren't the same. Dogs use their right and left nostrils differently depending on whether the smell is new or familiar. They start sniffing with the right side, and if it is familiar or a good smell (such as food), they shift to the left nostril. If the scent is new or threatening, they switch back to using only the right nostril. This behavior is connected to how dogs' brains process incoming information.

ASIAN ELEPHANT

What's going on inside? Asian elephants test their trunks.

Elephant trunks start developing early in gestation because they are essential to elephant survival immediately after birth. The trunk is a highly tactile, or touch-sensitive, body part and can feel pressure as soft as a light brush against the skin. This appendage has special sensing cells called Pacinian corpuscles, like layers of an onion filled with gel. These unique cells expand the elephant's ability to "hear" even very low vibrations and light pressures.

The trunk can be seen when the fetus is slightly over two and a half months old. After about twelve months in the womb (half of their gestation), the fetus can reach up and over its head with its trunk. It also practices curling its trunk into its mouth, which is the movement the elephant will use to feed itself after birth.

An Asian elephant has few sweat glands, and they are only near its feet. So its trunk is helpful for spraying dirt onto its back to keep cool. Dirt spraying may also help the elephant rid itself of pesky bugs.

Species: *Elephas maximus*
Common name: Asian elephant
Baby name: calf
Type: placental mammal
Chromosomes: 2n=56
Range: India and Southeast Asia
Gestation: twenty to twenty-four months (longest of any known mammal)
Number of wombmates: usually one, rarely two
Did you know? Asian elephants' trunks have about ninety thousand muscle fascicles, or bundles! They develop one fingerlike bump at the end that becomes one hundred times more sensitive than a human finger, allowing the elephant to pick up something as small as a peanut. When the elephant is full-grown, its muscular yet sensitive trunk will weigh as much as two adult men! The elephant can use its trunk to sense vibrations, smell, snorkel, drink, dust itself, push, pull, bathe, breathe, touch, and trumpet.

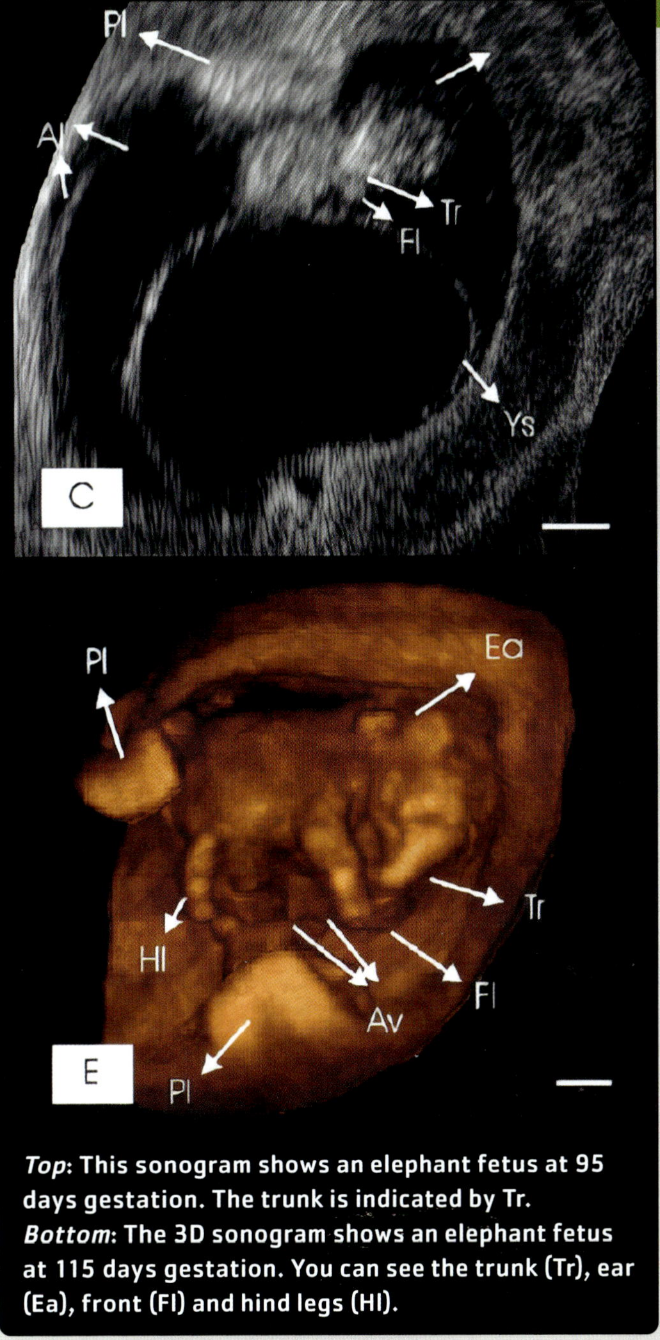

Top: This sonogram shows an elephant fetus at 95 days gestation. The trunk is indicated by Tr. *Bottom*: The 3D sonogram shows an elephant fetus at 115 days gestation. You can see the trunk (Tr), ear (Ea), front (Fl) and hind legs (Hl).

CHAPTER 4

CHOMP! BODY PARTS DESIGNED FOR INGESTING

We're at the final survival ability, and it's a big one: ingesting. Although animals require varying amounts of food and water, eating and drinking are essential to life. From the tiniest tree frog to the massive blue whale, organs and body systems can't function without water and nutrients. Here's why:

- **Energy supply.** Food gives animals energy. Their food is broken down in their digestive systems and converted into energy that powers everything their body needs to move, live, and grow.

Cows have one stomach with four compartments that work together to digest tough, fibrous plants such as grass. With the help of bacteria, microbes, enzymes, acids, and a lot of chewing, they break down food in multiple stages to get the most nutrients out of everything they ingest.

- **Building and repair.** Proteins from food help build and repair body tissues and cells.
- **Ongoing needs.** Minerals and vitamins in food help the body function in many ways, such as contracting muscles, keeping bones strong, clotting blood, and conducting nerve signals.
- **Reproduction.** Nutrients are needed to develop organs used in reproduction, produce eggs and sperm, and nourish young.

A giraffe's legs are longer than its neck, so it must spread its legs wide apart to reach the water to drink. This is a dangerous position because the giraffe's vision is limited so it is vulnerable to attack by predators.

- **Hydration.** Whether they drink or get water from their food, animals need water to break down food and transport nutrients, eliminate waste through urine and feces, and keep cells working. In some cases, such as dogs panting to cool off, they must replace water lost by regulating their body temperature.

Here's the kicker: Unlike humans, animals can't grow their own food or go get it from a grocery store. They must search their environment to find their resources. This hunt uses up their energy. If animals spend too much energy looking for food and water, they won't have enough energy to survive. It's the teeter-totter of the animal world.

Growing the body parts designed to help a creature ingest is essential work. Let's see how three animals accomplish it.

MAMUSHI SNAKE

What's going on inside? Mamushi snake forms its fangs.

The snakelet has the fangs it needs to hunt and live on its own from birth! As the snake strikes its prey, special glands in its mouth release toxic venom through these hollow teeth. Within minutes, the venom kills the prey (rodents such as chipmunks and squirrels, small birds, lizards, and insects) and the snake swallows its lunch whole. Eventually, stomach acids digest the meal.

Tiny fangs appear in the mamushi snake's mouth at the end of its gestation. The fangs grow down from inside its upper jaw. Usually, two fangs are on each side. Shortly after the fangs form, the rest of the teeth appear on the snake's bottom jaw.

The mamushi snake is well camouflaged among the leaves and debris on the ground. This adaptation helps it stay out of sight as it waits to ambush its prey.

Species: *Gloydius blomhoffii*
Common name: mamushi snake
Baby name: snakelet
Type: live-birth reptile
Chromosomes: 2n=36
Range: Japan, Korea, and China
Gestation: two to three months, depending on environmental conditions
Number of wombmates: up to twelve
Did you know? Mamushi snake fangs grow to be about 0.2 inches (5 mm) long—about the length of a pencil eraser. They are thin with sharp points on the end. They puncture skin so quickly and easily that some people who have been bitten said it felt more like a splinter than a snakebite! But recovery from the venomous bite can take several days in the hospital. It's no wonder feeling better takes a while. Mamushi snake venom is designed to dissolve the prey's body inside the snake's stomach, so it is easier to digest. Unlike our teeth, these fangs are replaced throughout the snake's life as needed. If one falls out, another is ready to move into position and deliver a venomous piercing.

See the mamushi snake fetus develop its fangs and features over time.

GREAT WHITE SHARK

What's going on inside? The great white shark transforms its teeth.

Great white sharks grow two kinds of teeth in the uterus, one type when they are younger and another as they get closer to birth. The first set—the embryonic teeth—are small pegs. They don't have a root in the jaw, and only some of them stick up. These teeth help the embryo break open its egg case and eat undeveloped eggs for food.

As the shark fetus grows older and larger, the baby teeth fall out. The fetus swallows some. These teeth are replaced by bigger, rigid, jagged-edged versions—similar to adult teeth—which the great white shark will need to rip apart its prey after it's born.

A great white shark breaks the surface displaying its rows of sharp teeth.

Species: *Carcharodon carcharias*
Common name: great white shark
Baby name: pup
Type: live-birth fish
Chromosomes: 2n=82
Range: all major temperate oceans around the world
Gestation: about twelve months
Number of wombmates: two to twelve
Did you know? An adult great white shark has about three hundred sharp, jagged teeth in its mouth at once. The upper teeth are more jagged for holding on to prey, and the lower teeth are sharper for cutting. Several rows of teeth grow in and fall out as they become dull or broken like a vending machine moving the next item forward if one slot is empty. A great white shark could go through up to twenty thousand teeth in its lifetime!

Top: This great white shark fetus has its mouth open.
Left: This close-up of a great white shark shows its developing baby teeth.

DOMESTIC CHICKEN

What's going on inside? The chicken begins its beak.

You probably know a chicken uses its beak for gathering food. But you might not know how this structure helps the bird find exactly the right size and type of food. The beak is a complex sensory organ with nerves that feel pain, temperature, and pressure.

The beak can be seen on the developing embryo's face on the third day of incubation. It is composed of keratin, a protein produced by the body. The upper (maxilla) and lower (mandible) features are developed by day ten, and the beak hardens. Around this time, nerve endings grow in the beak, so it develops a sense of touch. A special group of tiny sensors called the bill tip organ at the end of the beak will help the chicken feel very precisely.

By day twenty, the embryo is in the correct position to hatch. It breaks an air cell in the egg with its beak and uses its lungs to begin breathing air for the first time. (Now that it breathes, it is known as a chick instead of an embryo.) A temporary "egg tooth" on the tip of the

A flock of hens forage for food with their beaks.

beak develops. This helps the chick break through the eggshell and falls off shortly after it hatches.

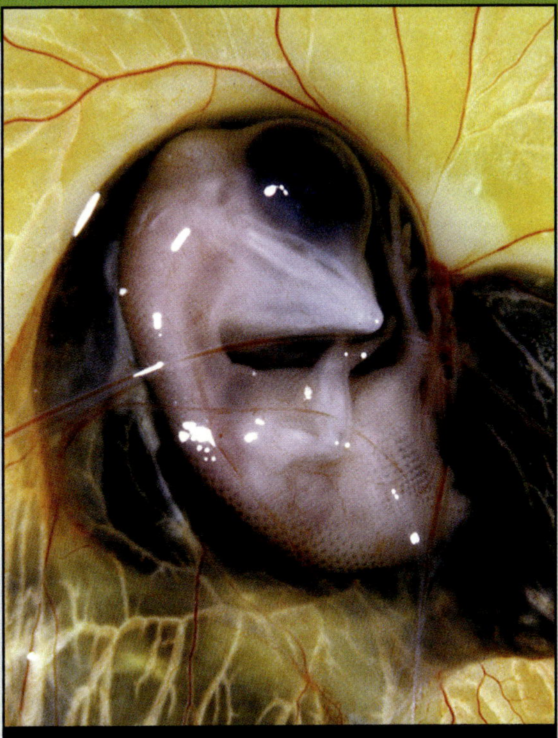

This domestic chicken fetus is nine days old developing inside an egg. Its beak is already forming.

Species: *Gallus gallus domesticus*
Common name: domestic chicken
Baby name: chick
Type: bird
Chromosomes: 2n=78
Range: worldwide
Gestation: twenty-one days
Number of wombmates: one per egg
Did you know? When fully grown, the chicken's beak will be a crucial tool, like the Swiss Army knife of body parts. The chicken will use it to find food, build a nest, explore its surroundings, drink, and clean its feathers. It can even use its beak as a weapon to defend itself or show dominance. And what about that loud cock-a-doodle-doo that roosters are famous for? The position and movement of a rooster's beak changes the pitch and volume of nature's alarm clock.

Female chickens, known as hens, can lay eggs without mating with a rooster. Since these eggs have not been fertilized with male reproductive cells (sperm), they cannot grow into a chick. But the eggs are safe to eat, and people around the world use eggs as a food source. The demand for eggs and chickens as a food source is so high that domestic chickens, which live with humans, outnumber any other bird species on Earth.

DIFFERENT IS GOOD: GESTATIONAL OUTLIERS

While many animals fit into neat categories of baby development, many others make us wonder. Meet the platypus, wallaby, and seahorse. These animals are entirely different from one another, yet they share one trait: all have unique gestations.

- The platypus is one of very few mammals that lay eggs. The female incubates them by curling around them and using her body to keep them warm.
- Wallabies are marsupials, mammals that grow babies differently than most. Marsupials give birth to an immature live baby that continues its development for months outside the womb, typically in a pouch on the mother's belly.

The platypus is a mash-up of unique structures with a beaverlike tail, webbed feet, and a duck bill.

- Female seahorses transfer their eggs into a specialized pouch on the male's body! The male then fertilizes the eggs within the pouch and carries them until they hatch. Once the young seahorses are fully developed, the male gives birth to live offspring.

While we may not know why some animals have such unique systems, we can study them to learn more about their developmental processes. Let's explore more about these outliers.

PLATYPUS

What's going on inside? Platypus prepares its paddle power.

From the earliest stage, the forelimbs and hind limbs are shaped differently from each other. They begin to develop when the embryo is inside its soft-shelled uterine egg. As the embryo grows, the footpads separate into digits. Eventually, its hind feet develop to look like duck feet, but they point backward. Its front feet will grow claws and will be able to grasp objects. They will also have webbing that continues past the ends of their claws and folds back when the platypus walks on land. The front and back feet will allow the pup to climb and paddle with extra force.

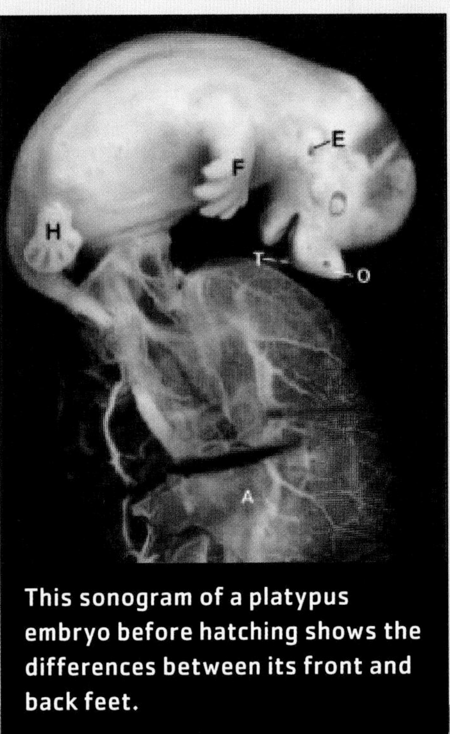

This sonogram of a platypus embryo before hatching shows the differences between its front and back feet.

Species: *Ornithorhynchus anatinus*
Common name: platypus
Baby name: nestling, puggle, or platypus
Type: monotreme
Chromosomes: 2n=54
Range: southeastern Australia and Tasmania

Gestation: inside the mother, likely up to twelve days, ten to twelve days outside the mother in the egg

Number of wombmates: usually two to three per litter

Did you know? A platypus is the only mammal with a bill. They spend most of their lives pulling their bodies through the water instead of walking. So, their limbs sprout from the sides of their bodies like a lizard's instead of under their bodies like a lion's.

TAMMAR WALLABY

What's going on inside? Tammar wallabies exercise early.

About three days before it is born, when it is only about the size of a jellybean, a tammar wallaby prepares for a journey! It stretches its tiny forelimbs up and down and opens and closes its handlike paws. All this movement builds muscle strength. The wallaby is born through the cloaca near the base of the mother's tail. Immediately, the wallaby's paws grasp its mom's belly hair, and its forelimbs pull its whole body up, up, up and into Mom's pouch. Living is good in the pouch. For eight to nine months, the joey suckles its mother's milk and increases its weight by two thousand times! In comparison, human babies only increase their weight by three times during their first year.

A tammar wallaby and her joey

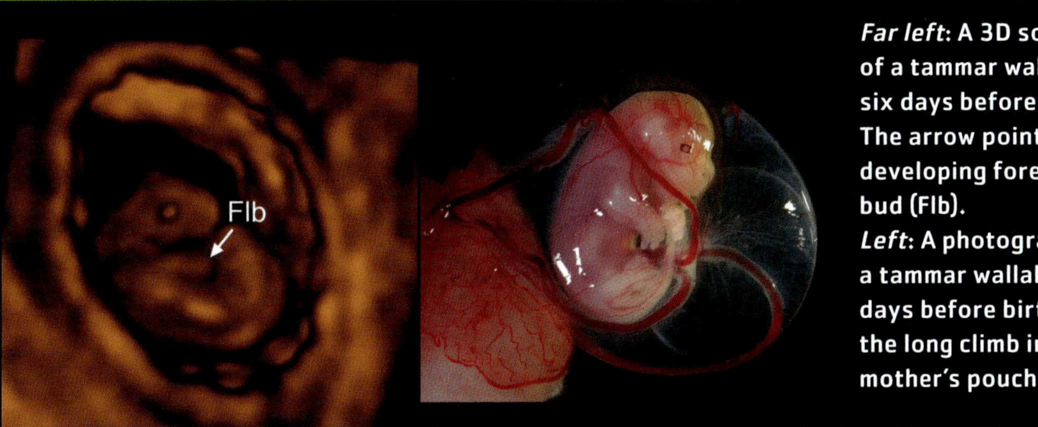

Far left: A 3D sonogram of a tammar wallaby six days before birth. The arrow points to the developing forelimb bud (Flb).
Left: A photograph of a tammar wallaby two days before birth and the long climb into its mother's pouch.

Species: *Macropus eugenii*
Common name: tammar wallaby
Baby name: joey
Range: south and western Australia and New Zealand
Gestation: twenty-five to twenty-eight days in the womb, eight to nine months in the pouch
Type: marsupial
Chromosomes: 2n=16
Number of wombmates: usually none
Did you know? Other animals practice their moves in utero too. Foals kick and lambs stretch. But the tammar wallaby begins its arm strengthening program when it is much younger and less mature than other animals. Eventually, these strong forelimbs will help wallabies grab food, groom themselves, "cuff" (hit) unfriendly wallabies, and dig shallow ditches for napping.

The tammar wallaby mother carries her growing joey in one of her two uteruses. Unlike most mammals, the joey is not attached to its mother by an umbilical cord. At about day twenty-six, the fetus is born, and right away, it must crawl up the mother's long belly and down inside her pouch to latch onto a teat, receive its mother's milk, and finish growing in the pouch for eight to nine months.

BIG-BELLY SEAHORSE

What's going on inside? The big-belly seahorse expands its eyesight.

The eyes of big-belly seahorses begin to form early, giving them enough time to develop good vision by the time they are born. The eyes have pigment within the brood pouch in fourteen to seventeen days. When the fetus is born in another two weeks, its eyes are open and watching the world. The eyes must be open—seahorses don't have eyelids! Each eye moves on its own and helps the tiny seahorse spot prey and locate danger around it.

Species: *Hippocampus abdominalis*
Common name: big-belly seahorse
Baby name: fry
Type: live-birth fish

A male big-belly seahorse has a special growing pouch to hold developing fry.

FISH FATHERS

Almost all animals develop inside their mothers. But fish dads of a few species, such as sea dragons, pipefish, and seahorses, provide the womb! In the Syngnathidae fish family, the male carries developing embryos in his brood pouch. Each seahorse embryo develops in its own tiny nook. Fathers supply fats for energy and calcium so the embryos can build their tiny skeletons and bony body rings under their skin. With up to one thousand or more embryos in one brood pouch, no wonder seahorse dads have such big bellies! Each tiny seahorse is born live and ready to fend for itself.

Chromosomes: 2n=21
Range: ocean waters near New Zealand and Australia
Gestation: about one month
Number of wombmates: up to one thousand
Did you know? Seahorses have excellent vision. Unlike most animals (including humans), who can only look in one direction at a time, seahorses can look forward and backward at the same time! Because their long snout is used to vacuum up their prey—not to smell danger—seahorses rely on their eyesight to keep themselves safe.

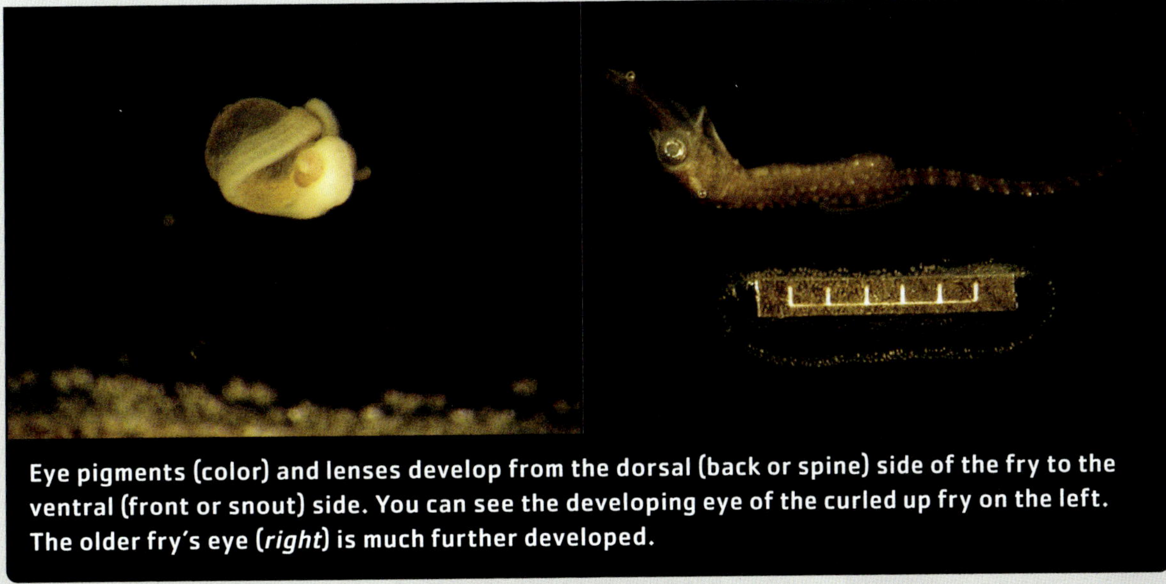

Eye pigments (color) and lenses develop from the dorsal (back or spine) side of the fry to the ventral (front or snout) side. You can see the developing eye of the curled up fry on the left. The older fry's eye (*right*) is much further developed.

CONCLUSION

ONE QUESTION, MANY ANSWERS

Why is it important for people to understand how animals begin their lives?

I focused on this question while researching and writing this book. It was a big thought, and eventually, I found many answers. Here are some:

- **Life is amazing.** Understanding how animals start shows us how complicated and remarkable new life is.
- **We're all connected.** When we learn about how animals grow, we see how similar human development is to them in the early stages. This connection can make us care more about protecting animals and their habitats.
- **We might be inspired.** Learning about how animals develop could spark investigations or a career as a scientist or veterinarian. It might inspire us to study anatomy, genetics, or medical science.
- **There's still a lot to discover.** For instance, scientists are still trying to understand why embryos and species have developed the way they have. They wonder how certain traits have evolved to help animals survive. They explore how external factors (such as climate change or pollution) affect embryos as they grow. Learning more could help us protect endangered

animals or species that are almost extinct such as northern white rhinos.

- **Knowledge can be transferred.** Studying how animals grow can lead to discoveries in medical care for humans. For example, a field of science called regenerative medicine explores how animal embryos regrow body tissues. Understanding this may help scientists find treatments for human problems, such as healing injured organs or tissues.

Do you have more answers about why it is important to understand animal beginnings? Go ahead and give it some thought. Your big idea could be just what the world needs.

A veterinarian feeds a baby meerkat.

AUTHOR'S NOTE

Species: *Homo sapiens*
Common name: Carrie A. Pearson (human)
Baby name: infant
Type: placental mammal
Chromosomes: 2n=46
Range: around the world
Gestation: about nine months
Number of wombmates: none
Did you know? During the COVID-19 pandemic, I watched the stage play *Hamilton* on television six times. I loved everything about it . . . the plot, history information, actors, and music. On the sixth viewing, I listened to the song "The Room Where It Happens" (again), but this time, I had a light bulb moment. I envisioned writing a book called *The Womb Where It Happens* that would include the latest research and understanding of animal beginnings. It would combine my love of science, babies, and animals and share a world that most of us don't know or think about but is happening around us every second of every day. Although we didn't keep the original title, now you know how the idea for this book was born!

HOW TO NAME YOUR BABY

Choosing the right name for a new baby can be tricky! What if you are a scientist who has discovered an animal that has never been documented before? How would you let other people know what kind of animal it is? Binomial nomenclature to the rescue! This system of naming helps scientists all over the world classify and identify animals and plants. Each living organism gets two (bi) names (nomial). Here is the binomial nomenclature for humans: *Homo sapiens*. It combines two Latin words, *Hom*, meaning "human," and *sapiens*, meaning "wise."

BEST BABY GIFTS FOR ANIMALS

Just like human babies, animal babies need the right conditions to grow, stay safe, and become strong adults. Protecting their food and water sources, their natural habitats, and the animals themselves gives them the best chance. Here are some real-world conservation efforts and things we can do to help:

1. Protect Food and Water Sources

Organizations like the African Wildlife Foundation (https://www.awf.org/) are restoring watering holes that have dried up due to climate change and are helping baby elephants, rhinos, and zebras survive.

What You Can Do:

- Support efforts that preserve ecosystems that animals need to live.
- Reduce plastic waste to keep rivers and oceans clean. Participate in beach and park clean-ups to remove trash that harms baby animals like sea turtles and otters.
- Walk, bike, or carpool to reduce carbon emissions that contribute to climate change.
- Choose to use sustainable products (like recycled paper and responsibly sourced food) to protect land and water.

2. Provide Cover and Protection for Young Animals

The National Audubon Society (https://www.audubon.org/) and local wildlife groups track and protect nesting areas. Healthy forests and prairies provide safe nesting sites for eagles, owls, and songbirds.

What You Can Do:

- Keep fallen logs, leaves, and native plants in your yard to provide shelter for growing animals.
- Avoid using pesticides that harm the insects baby birds eat.

3. Protect Wildlife from Poaching and Illegal Trade

Groups like Save the Rhino (https://www.savetherhino.org/) rescue orphaned baby rhinos and prepare them to live in the wild.

What You Can Do:

- Never buy products made from illegal wildlife materials (ivory, exotic animal skins, etc.).
- Support anti-poaching efforts by donating to reputable conservation groups.

Every small action helps give baby animals a good start in life.

GLOSSARY

alleles: different versions of a gene inherited from the biological mother and father. They work together to help determine the offspring's traits or characteristics, such as eye color.

baby schema: a group of features such as a round face, big eyes, a small nose and eyes, and a high forehead that humans (and some studied animals) think are cute.

chromosomes: tiny, threadlike structures inside a cell's nucleus that instruct how an organism is built and works. They also pass these instructions from one cell to another.

embryo: a bundle of cells that can grow into the major structures and systems of an animal's body.

evolution: the process by which new species or populations of living things develop and change over generations

fetus: when the embryo has developed basic body structures and begins to have body parts that look like an adult of its kind

gametes: reproductive or sex cells in an organism

genes: pieces of information found on chromosomes. Genes code for or guide the expression of the organism's traits, features, or functions.

gestation: the period of time an animal develops inside its mother or egg before being born or hatching

ingesting: the process of taking in something, usually food-related

karyotype: a digital picture of all the chromosomes in a cell arranged in pairs by number

live birth: when an animal is born directly from its mother, without being inside an eggshell

marsupial: a type of mammal such as the kangaroo, wallaby, and opossum that carries its fetus in a pouch on the mother's abdomen while the baby finishes developing

meiosis: a cell-dividing process that forms gametes

mitosis: the process of somatic cells dividing and replicating

monotreme: a type of mammal, such as the platypus and echidna, that lays eggs instead of giving birth to live babies like most mammals

placental mammal: a type of mammal, such as a bat, dolphin, or human, that develops inside its mother and gets food and oxygen through a pancake-shaped organ called the placenta attached to the mother

somatic cells: cells in an organism that form the body's tissues and organs

sonogram: an image produced from an ultrasound

zygote: a fertilized cell formed when two gametes merge

SELECTED BIBLIOGRAPHY

Baker Institute for Animal Health. "Canine Embryonic Atlas Online." Cornell University College of Veterinary Medicine, n.d.

Borgi, Marta, Irene Cogliati-Dezza, Victoria Brelsford, Kerstin Meints, and Francesca Cirulli. "Baby Schema in Human and Animal Faces Induces Cuteness Perception and Gaze Allocation in Children." *Frontiers in Psychology*, April 19, 2014.

Drews, Barbara, Kathleen Roellig, Brandon R. Menzies, Geoff Shaw, Ina Buentjen, Catherine A. Herbert, Thomas B. Hildebrandt, and Marilyn B. Renfree. "Ultrasonography of Wallaby Prenatal Development Shows That the Climb to the Pouch Begins in Utero." *Scientific Reports*, 2013.

Eveleth, Rose. "There Are 37.2 Trillion Cells in Your Body." *Smithsonian Magazine*, October 24, 2013.

Hughes, R. Leon, and Leslie S. Hall. "Early Development and Embryology of the Platypus." *Philosophical Transactions of the Royal Society* B 353, no. 1372 (1998): 1101–1114.

Hildebrandt, Thomas, Barbara Drews, Ann P. Gaeth, Frank Goeritz, Robert Hermes, Dennis Schmitt, Charlie Gray et al. "Foetal Age Determination and Development in Elephants." *Proceedings: Biological Sciences* 274, no. 1608 (2006): 323-331.

Hill, Mark. "Bat Development." Embryology education and research website, n.d., https://embryology.med.unsw.edu.au/embryology/index.php?title=Bat_Development.

"The Human Genome Project." Genome.gov, n.d.

Shimada, Kenshu. "Teeth of Embryos in Lamniform Sharks (Chondrichthyes: Elasmobranchii)." *Environmental Biology of Fishes* 63 (2002): 309-319.

Skawiński, Tomasz, Grzegorz Skórzewski, and Bartosz Borczyk. "Embryonic Development and Perinatal Skeleton in a Limbless, Viviparous Lizard, *Anguis Fragilis* (Squamata: Anguimorpha)." *PeerJ* 9, no. 6 (2021): e11621.

Sommer, Stefan, Camilla M. Whittington, and Anthony B. Wilson. "Standardised Classification of Pre-Release Development in Male-Brooding Pipefish, Seahorses, and Seadragons (Family Syngnathidae)." *BMC Developmental Biology* 12, no. 39 (2012).

"Stages in Chick Embryo Development." Mississippi State University Extension Service, n.d.

Štěrba, Oldřich, Milan Klima, and Bernd Schildger. *Embryology of Dolphins: Staging and Ageing of Embryos and Fetuses of Some Cetaceans. Advances in Anatomy, Embryology and Cell Biology*. Berlin: Springer, 2000.

Tarlach, Gemma. "Why Babies Are So Cute—And Why We React the Way We Do." *Discover*, May 9, 2020.

Tokita, Masayoshi, and Hiroki Watanabe. "Embryonic Development of the Japanese Mamushi, Gloydius Blomhoffii (Squamata: Serpentes: Viperidae: Crotalinae)." *Current Herpetology* 38, no. 1 (2019): 6–13.

University of Western Australia, ed. "Why Do All Animal Embryos Look The Same?" Lab + Life Science LabOnline, n.d.

Wrenn, Joan T., and Norman K. Wesells. "The Early Development of Mystacial Vibrissae in the Mouse." *Journal of Embryology and Experimental Morphology* 83 (1984): 137–156.

Young, Carly. "I Am an Animal Embryologist." San Diego Zoo Wildlife Alliance, April 23, 2021.

MORE TO EXPLORE

BOOKS

Albrechtová, Jana, Radka Piro, and Lida Larina. *Foldout Anatomy: An Interactive Look Inside Humans and Animals*. Fresno, CA: Bushel & Peck Books, 2022.

Collard, Sneed B., and Steve Jenkins. *Making Animal Babies*. Boston: Houghton Mifflin, 2000.

Fisher, Carolyn. *Cells: An Owner's Handbook*. New York: Beach Lane Books, 2019.

Michels, Dia L., and Andrew Barthelmes. *If My Mom Were a Platypus: Mammal Babies and Their Mothers*. Washington: Science, Naturally!, 2014.

Sims, Michael. *In the Womb: Animals*. Washington, DC: National Geographic, 2009.

VIDEOS

"A Baby Dolphin Is Born, Dolphins of Shark Bay"
https://www.youtube.com/watch?v=PMxbZh2CBjk
Watch a newborn dolphin learn how to breath air and swim at the same time.

"Animals in the Womb"
https://www.youtube.com/watch?v=XaZW7bbmc9I
This video combines real video footage and computer graphics to show the process of reproduction and gestation for an Asian elephant, golden retriever, and dolphin.

"How Do Bats Land Upside Down?"
https://www.youtube.com/watch?v=342Y_040f1Y
Watch a bat land upside down and learn how they use inertia to make it happen.

"In the Womb: Animal Babies"
https://www.youtube.com/watch?v=3Jo7WfH_D8o
Learn about the gestation experiences of a dog, lion, meerkat, and elephant.

"Smithsonian Channel: Great Snakes (2015) Documentary *Mamushi*"
https://www.youtube.com/watch?v=utx-rYYqK5M
See how a mamushi snake finds its prey and strikes with its fangs.

Live Stream Platypus Cam at the San Diego Zoo
https://sdzsafaripark.org/cams/platypus-cam
The San Diego Zoo is the only place outside of Australia where platypus live.

INDEX

Photo Acknowledgments

Image Credits: Anup Shah/Getty Images, pp. 5, 26; LittleDogKorat/Shutterstock, p. 6 (top); Lopolo/Shutterstock, p. 6 (bottom); Rawpixel.com/Shutterstock, p. 7 (top); Prostock-studio/Shutterstock, p. 7 (middle); Ephert/Wikimedia Commons (CC BY-SA 4.0), p. 7 (bottom); Dhananjaya Bandara JM/500px/Getty Images, p. 8; Tetiana Zhabska/Alamy, p. 9; fatido/Getty Images, p. 11; Pikovit/Shutterstock, pp. 12–13; Kanyanat wongsa/Shutterstock, p. 15; © Heidi and Hans-Juergen Koch/Minden Pictures, p. 18 (top); Natalia Sinjushina & Evgeniy Meyke/Shutterstock, p. 18 (bottom); Martyn Colbeck/Getty Images, p. 19; Image by Ruben Moreno Montoliu/Getty Images, p. 20; Roland Seitre/naturepl.com, p. 22; E.R. Degginger/Alamy, p. 23; Carly Young, San Diego Zoo Wildlife Alliance, p. 24; SAM YEH/AFP/Getty Images, p. 25; nikpal/Getty Images, p. 27; Ivan Kuzmin/Alamy, p. 28; Chris Cretekos and Richard Behringer, p. 29 (left); imageBROKER.com/Alamy, p. 30; Thewissen, J. G. M. "Highlights of Cetacean Embryology." *Aquatic Mammals*, vol. 44, no. 6 (2018): 591–602. DOI: 10.1578/AM.44.6.2018.591, p. 31; Ian Thraves/Alamy, p. 32; Skawiński T, Skórzewski G, Borczyk B. Embryonic development and perinatal skeleton in a limbless, viviparous lizard, *Anguis fragilis* (Squamata: Anguimorpha)," *PeerJ* 9, no. 6 (2021): e11621, https://doi.org/10.7717/peerj.11621 (CC-BY 4.0), p. 33; Picture by Tambako the Jaguar/Getty Images, p. 34; Santiago Urquijo/Getty Images, p. 36; © 2010 Paudyal et al., licensee BioMed Central Ltd. (CC BY 2.0), p. 37 (bottom); Iwabuchi, Tokuro, and Paul F. Goetinck. "Syndecan-4 Dependent FGF Stimulation of Mouse Vibrissae Growth." *Mechanisms of Development* 123, no. 11 (Nov. 2006): 792–800. Elsevier, https://doi.org/10.1016/j.mod.2006.08.003, p. 37 (top); John McKeen/Getty Images, p. 38; Baker Institute for Animal Health, p. 39; ephotocorp/Alamy, p. 40; Drews, B., et al. "Early Embryo Development in the Elephant Assessed by Serial Ultrasound Examinations." *Theriogenology* 69, no. 9 (June 2008): 1120-1128 , p. 41; Marcel ter Bekke/Getty Images, p. 42; Martin Harvey/Getty Images, p. 43; 23frogger/Shutterstock, p. 44; Masayoshi Tokita and Hiroki Watanabe, p.45; David Fleetham/Alamy, p. 46; Sato, Keiichi, et al. "How Great White Sharks Nourish Their Embryos to a Large Size: Evidence of Lipid Histotrophy in Lamnoid Shark Reproduction." *Biology Open* 5, no. 5 (2016): 607–610, https://doi.org/10.1242/bio.017939. Accessed 21 Mar. 2025. (CC BY 3.0), p. 47; georgeclerk/Getty Images, p. 48; E.R. Degginger/Science Source, p. 49; Christopher Bellette/Alamy, p. 50; Hughes and Hall, "Early Development and Embryology of the Platypus," *Philosophical Transactions of the Royal Society* B 353, no. 1372 (1998): 1101–1114. © 1998 The Royal Society, p. 51; Geraldine Buckley/Alamy, p. 52; Drews, Barbara, et al. "Ultrasonography of Wallaby Prenatal Development Shows That the Climb to the Pouch Begins in Utero." *Scientific Reports* 3, no. 1458 (2013), https://doi.org/10.1038/srep01458. Accessed 21 Mar. 2025. (CC BY-NC-ND 3.0), p. 53; Susan E. Degginger/Science Source, p. 54; Stefan Sommer/University of Zurich, p. 55 (all); Darya Komarova/Getty Images, p. 57. Design Element: Rost9/Shutterstock.

Cover: Dorit Hockman/Science Source. Dorit Bar-Zakay/Getty Images.